T0326577

The Communicating Principal

The Communicating Principal

Practical Strategies for School Leaders

Trinette Marquis
Natalie A. Nash

ROWMAN & LITTLEFIELD
Lanham • Boulder • New York • London

Published by Rowman & Littlefield
An imprint of The Rowman & Littlefield Publishing Group, Inc.
4501 Forbes Boulevard, Suite 200, Lanham, Maryland 20706
www.rowman.com

86-90 Paul Street, London EC2A 4NE, United Kingdom

British Library Cataloguing in Publication Information Available

Library of Congress Cataloging-in-Publication Data

Names: Marquis, Trinette, author. | Nash, Natalie A., 1970- author.
Title: The communicating principal : practical strategies for school leaders / Trinette Marquis, Natalie A. Nash.
Description: Lanham : Rowman & Littlefield Publishing, [2022] | Summary: "Strong campus communication is the foundation of motivated and inspired staff, connected families, supportive community members, and engaged partners. Through stories, best-practice guidelines, and real-world tips and checklists, The Communicating Principal gives school leaders the tools they need to share their vision and transform their campus"—Provided by publisher.
Identifiers: LCCN 2021032069 (print) | LCCN 2021032070 (ebook) | ISBN 9781475862621 (cloth) | ISBN 9781475862638 (paperback) | ISBN 9781475862645 (epub)
Subjects: LCSH: School principals. | Communication in education. | Educational leadership. | School management and organization.
Classification: LCC LB2831.9 .M356 2022 (print) | LCC LB2831.9 (ebook) | DDC 371.2/012—dc23
LC record available at https://lccn.loc.gov/2021032069
LC ebook record available at https://lccn.loc.gov/2021032070

Between the time we started working together on this book and the day we completed it, the world changed. Seemingly overnight, teachers, support staff, and school leaders were asked to do the impossible—completely reimagine teaching and learning.

In the spring of 2020, teachers everywhere became learners themselves, figuring out new technologies, online resources, and how to engage students from a distance. School support staff kept students fed with curbside pick-ups and technology staff figured out how to get devices and connections to the teachers and learners that needed them.

Perhaps during the COVID-19 pandemic more than any other time, our schools became a central hub, supporting students, families, and communities through the uncertainty. This book is dedicated to all of those committed individuals who worked so hard to meet the needs of students around the country. Thank you for all you do every day.

Contents

Foreword   ix

Acknowledgments   xi

Introduction   xv

1 The Case for Effective Communication: The
   Communication Principle   1

Part I: Research   9

2 Research as a Foundation   11

3 Qualitative Research   25

Part II: Planning   33

4 Understanding Your Audiences   35

5 Planning Your Work   41

6 Messaging   49

Part III: Implementation   57

7 Communication Channels   59

8 Social Media   67

9 Supportive Systems   75

10 Crisis Communication   81

11 Working with the Media   91

12 Internal Communication   101

13 Culture Building   109

14 Customer Service   117

Part IV: Evaluating   **125**

15 Measuring Your Work   127

16 Data Collection   135

17 Analytics   145

Part V: In Closing   **153**
  18 Leading   155

Appendix A: Online Supplemental Materials   165
Appendix B: Employee, Community, Family, and Student
    Engagement Ideas   167
Glossary   169
Additional Resources   173
About the Authors   175

Foreword

My own journey to becoming a school leader took many twists and turns. As the daughter of two public school teachers who vowed never to work in education, here I sit after a career in journalism. What I probably would have told you back then is that media training would help you communicate more effectively. What I have since learned is that media relations is not enough. In fact, the majority of school leaders have no access to media markets to help with this task.

Like many other roles in your school, this, too, is one you have to take up. School principals are a visible part of many local communities; you can use that role to help champion the cause for children.

Being a school leader amid a polarized environment during a pandemic is not for the faint of heart. It takes a special skill to be able to navigate these trying times, but you've taken the first step by opening this book. Let's face it: you are at the intersection of where your district's mission meets the necessary action to fulfill it, and it's your leadership that will make that happen.

Unfortunately, there is no playbook to tell you what to do when a particular situation occurs. However, what you are equipping yourself with is a framework that guides you into better decision-making away from the hot topics which bring you here today. The role of a school principal is more than just one of an instructional leader—you must become a savvy communicator to help guide your community through these times. *The Communicating Principal: Practical Strategies for School Leaders* will help you do just that.

The reality is that not every school or district is able to employ a full-time school public relations practitioner; however, every school and district has a need for an effective plan and process to communicate with stakeholders—from the mundane to the mishaps. This is a lesson I learned when I tried to help school leaders to understand why this work matters. They couldn't until the crisis arrived, and by then it was too late. That's why I spend time coaching school leaders on the cause and effect of a powerful school public relations program. It makes the work of leading a school easier when you have others bought into your system to help.

As you prepare for the journey into school PR as a school leader, know that there is a network of support available to you. Throughout this book, you will likely find case studies from systems who are doing the work. Take note of the issue and the response and if you need more help, take the time to find their contact information to ask questions. What you will find is what I already know: there is a community of school public relations practitioners who are readily willing to share what they have learned to help you get better.

Lesley Bruinton, APR
National School Public Relations Association president

Acknowledgments

Educators and those who work to support them are some of the most talented and dedicated individuals on the planet. It is also an incredibly generous community that supports one another.

This book is an example of that spirit—despite the intensity of the year that all of our colleagues had experienced in the midst of a pandemic and changing circumstances, so many stepped up when we were looking for ideas and feedback and put countless hours into making this text infinitely better.

We want to thank everyone who listened, encouraged, and challenged us, including the following public relations professionals and school principals/superintendents: Cara Adney, Angela Griffin Ankhelyi, APR, John Baggett, Diedre Barlow, Krystyna Baumgartner, APR, Dr. Rose Borunda, Lesley Bruinton, APR, Curtis Campbell, Zachery Fountain, Kate Hazarian, Amy Jacobs, Grace Jens, Cathy Kedjidjian, APR, Heather McGowan, APR, Robert Myers, Michelle Pechette, Carla Pereira, APR, Xanthi Soriano and Amy Woodman.

—Natalie and Trinette

My sisters and dad are my foundation. They are my biggest cheerleaders, helping me believe I can do anything I set out to do. I wish more of our young people had that kind of support. School has also been a place of strength for me. No matter what else was happening in life, there were people in elementary, junior high, high school, and college that helped me get through hard things and focus on learning.

My time at Twin Rivers USD gave me the freedom to develop a new district and (extreme!) challenges to discover how much I could grow professionally. Despite dealing with some incredibly difficult situations, I wouldn't trade the experience for anything.

Since going out on my own, I have been blessed with an array of client projects that have allowed me to see school communication from completely new perspectives. From large urban to small rural districts, the stakeholder research and campaign development and implementation gave me the confidence to write that I believe will be universally helpful.

When you are particularly lucky as a consultant, sometimes you get a client that feels like home—I'm grateful to have that in Escalon Unified School District and want to thank Ron Costa and his team for inviting me in and working with me to improve communication throughout the school community.

The other part of my professional life is teaching—it has given me the opportunity to see the communications function from a completely different lens. My experience in the classroom has given me a much greater appreciation for administrative leadership, culture, and internal communication. My love for my students and learning about their struggles has given me much greater insight about equity, bias, and connection.

At home, I owe a huge thanks to Bill Morales. This book didn't happen without his support, his stepping up to take care of everything else in life so I could write and his reminders to me on the tough days that what I do matters.

Lastly, and certainly not least, the woman who jumped in on this crazy adventure with me! Natalie Nash brings a depth and storytelling talent to this project that really gives it heart and soul. I'm blessed to have a thought partner, fellow dreamer, and amazing friend like you.

—Trinette

I am forever grateful to my family who has taught me how to jump and leap, and soar, without fear of falling. To my parents, Rev. Dr. Frank and Patricia White, I'm still doing things I never thought possible because you both believed I could. To my big brother and sisters, Marcelino, Carlendia, and Maureen, thank you for love and devotion. To my loving Uncle George, although I never *actually* baked you that cake, I hope I've made you proud.

Special thanks to Ron Patton and Dr. Rochelle Clark for your mentorship, wisdom, and leadership. You exemplify the importance and necessity for thought-partnership. Terri Tobin, my work in equity wouldn't be possible without our rich history of hard conversations about race. You've taught me that we have so much more in common than what separates us. To past and present members of the Crete-Monee School District 201-U school board and district colleagues who value and support the importance of communication and stakeholder engagement. Stacey Elliott, my longtime webmaster/designer, thank you for your art and pictures that help my words make sense.

I'm incredibly grateful for my INSPRA Equity Task Force team: Jesse Chatz, Brett Clark, and Terri McHugh. I am so proud of the work we've done so far! Many thanks to INSPRA president, Carol Smith, for leading with vision and heart.

To my beautiful daughter Vivian Elise, thank you for knowing when I needed to hear, "You got this, Ma." Lastly, to the love of my life, Steven Nash. None of this could have been possible without your loving support. Thank you for reading drafts of this even when all you wanted to do was go play golf. It means the world to me, as do you.

And finally, to my writing partner, Trinette Marquis, who sees a world without boundaries, believes in the possibilities, and shares her love of learning with all those blessed to be in her presence. Thank you, my friend, for allowing me to take this journey with you.

—Natalie

Introduction

WHY THIS BOOK?

School communication has never been more difficult to navigate. Historical inequities, the growth in digital communication technologies, and a highly politicized political climate have increased the pressure on school leaders.

While most of the dedicated professionals who rise in the field are excellent educators, they may not always have the communication background or training needed to meet these unprecedented challenges.

This book is intended to provide guidance for the school or district leader who understands that communication is an essential element of student, staff, and campus success. Each chapter will provide a number of tips, templates, and resources to help save you time and help you be more effective in your efforts.

THE CASE FOR MORE COMMUNICATION

In the first chapter of this book, we build the case for effective campus-level communication with a discussion of the current educational environment, the impact of communication on student success, and the importance of campus and branding. This chapter is chock full of reasons to spend more time and energy on your communication strategy.

RPIE PROCESS

This book is organized by the public relations four-step process, including research, planning, implementation, and evaluation (RPIE). In each of the RPIE sections, the chapters can be read as individual reference guides, for example if you are needing additional information on social media (implementing section, chapter 7) or if you want to learn more about how to measure and report on communication outcomes (evaluation section, chapter 14). These chapters can also be read in sequence as a primer for effective school communication.

Each chapter opens with a story about how the chapter topic played out at a school site and ends with an "Ask & Answer" section to help provoke deeper thought about how the topic affects the reader's campus and additional steps they can take in their school community.

RESEARCH: CHAPTERS 2 AND 3

As the first step in the RPIE process, the first two chapters discuss the need for research in communication efforts, types of research, and tips for how to implement quick and easy quantitative and qualitative research methods in support of school communication.

PLANNING: CHAPTERS 4, 5, AND 6

Once the research is conducted, the results are analyzed and form the foundation for effective communication. While the planning steps may appear invisible to the outside world, they are the key to successful public relations efforts. Getting specific and targeted about audiences, messaging and tactics ensures your valuable time and resources are spent in the most effective ways possible.

IMPLEMENTATION: CHAPTERS 7 THROUGH 14

The most visible step in the four-step process, implementation is the video, the brochure, the social media post, or the email that is sent out. It is putting the plan into action. These chapters will take the reader through a discussion of different communication channel options, social media platforms, internal communication, and customer service. There is also a chapter on building the systems needed to ensure that communicating becomes an organizational expectation that is easy to do.

EVALUATION: CHAPTERS 15 THROUGH 17

The last step in the RPIE process is the one that most people forget. Once the communication campaign is over, we don't often think about reviewing its effectiveness. In many cases, we are not sure if we were successful or not. These chapters provide guidance on how to measure communication work and how to collect information and data to track effectiveness.

CLOSING

In the closing section of the book, we cover larger topics that don't fit within a specific step of the RPIE process, including leading, equity, and taking care of yourself. The closing section also contains a helpful glossary of terms as they relate to school communication and a section of resources for additional help and information.

From cheap and easy research methods, to tips for survey development, to systemic tracking and reporting ideas that will demonstrate the value of communication, it's in here. Our goal is to provide a book that can be referenced on an as-needed basis for special projects and issues, as well as provide an in-depth handbook for those wanting to improve their communication skills as an educational leader.

ONE

The Case for Effective Communication

The Communication Principle

The simple purpose of this book is this—improving schools by providing school leaders with the guidance and tips they need to be effective communicators. The underlying truth is that when principals are able to connect with stakeholders and create the conditions that support strong communication throughout the campus community, schools are better. They are better for students, better for staff, better for families, and ultimately better serve the long-term interests of the community.

As Harvard University Lecturer Dr. Karen Mapp argues in the Dual Capacity-Building Framework for Family-School Partnerships, school leaders who invest in family engagement see a robust return on a variety of levels. The Framework lays out the conditions that create the foundation for that engagement, including mutual trust, cultural responsiveness, respect, and collaboration—all facilitated by effective communication practices.

Strong campus communication results in motivated and inspired staff, connected families, supportive community members, and engaged partners. All of these layers combine to provide an environment of success for all students.

MOTIVATED AND INSPIRED STAFF

When staff (including support staff in the office, cafeteria, and grounds-keeping) understand the mission and values of the campus and their role in supporting it, they perform better and contribute to a more welcoming culture. When teachers are connected to each other, they share more

1

ideas and shared best practices, which improves teaching and learning. When they feel more connected to the school, they also become a potential marketing and promotional force, sharing the strengths of the campus within their spheres of influence.

CONNECTED FAMILIES

In John Hattie's book *Visible Learning*, he ranks 252 influences related to student achievement based on a review of nearly 800 meta-analyses. According to the list, meaningful parental involvement is highly impactful.

However, what exactly does that mean? One of the most important things a school staff can do is to start a conversation about the shared definition of family engagement. In the past, schools have been happy to welcome family members to campus to hold bake sales, make copies, or help staple packets. However, as educators explore meaningful engagement that truly impacts student learning, they are reimagining the concept and opportunities.

With the impact of COVID-19 in 2020, even more was learned about the impact of family members on learning. Students with a parent or other family member in the home who could assist and monitor were definitely at an advantage compared to peers without that support.

Even before COVID-19, students benefited from family members who were able to provide additional enrichment in the home, guide students through academic pathways and resources, and understand the complexities of applying to college and financial aid. Without this resource, some students fall behind or never gain the practical knowledge needed to navigate school and college options.

Mapp argues strong engagement practices invite families to participate in diverse roles; as co-creators of classroom content and activities, as academic supporters and encouragers in the classroom and at home, and as advocates for their child. This requires an upfront investment in effective family communication practices but yields dramatic increases in student learning and staff and family satisfaction.

Satisfied families talk about their experiences in their community. They tell neighbors, fellow athletic team parents, and friends about their school and how well it serves their child. That kind of word-of-mouth marketing is gold.

SUPPORTIVE COMMUNITY

Increased communication about the campus results in a more supportive community. That might look like higher attendance at athletic events and performances, which makes students feel great and increases the connection between schools and community members.

It also leads to stronger support at the ballot box. In many communities, a large percentage of the homeowners in a school neighborhood do not have a child that attends that school. When it comes to voting for facility bonds or approving budgets, the more positive stories they hear about the students and programs and the more personal experience they have with the campus, the more likely they are to support much-needed funding.

Like satisfied families, supportive community members can help build and sustain a school's positive reputation. For example, real estate agents answer questions all the time about area school districts. When they know and share great things about a school, it leads to increasing enrollment numbers.

Positive, consistent communication might also inspire some community members to step up and become engaged partners with the school. Business, political, and media partners can provide valuable additional resources for students in the form of funding, vocal support, materials, and opportunities.

LACK OF COMMUNICATION TRAINING

While most people would agree that it is helpful to have school principals who are great communicators, unfortunately aspiring administrators are rarely given enough training in the critical area. They may be wonderful educators, talented at identifying necessary academic interventions, and visionary in their approach to teaching and learning. However, a school leader who cannot effectively communicate that vision and unify people around it will have a difficult time making it a reality.

Schools are complex organizations with a variety of stakeholder groups that have a huge impact on the success of students. Effective communication practices are at the heart of understanding those groups and proactively engaging them to create the optimal conditions for learning.

POVERTY

Even before the recent pandemic, school leaders have faced unprecedented issues that complicate communication efforts. Among those are inequalities related to class, race, gender, and sexual orientation. Making those issues more difficult is the political climate which separates people and highlights differences rather than shared human experiences.

It is more important than ever that school leaders understand the larger environment in which their school is operating and create effective systems of communication that bring stakeholder groups together to tackle these challenges.

Official U.S. Census Bureau statistics estimate that 40 million persons, 12.3 percent of the total population, were poor in the United States in 2017. The global pandemic that struck in 2020 and continued into 2021 did nothing to help that figure. The United States (US) has the highest child poverty rates in the developed world.

A United Nations fifteen-day tour of Alabama, California, Puerto Rico, West Virginia, and Washington, D.C., in 2020 documented homelessness, unsafe sanitation, and sewage disposal practices, as well as police surveillance, overcriminalization, and harassment of the poor.

Many students, when they make it to school, are hungry, tired, stressed, and suffering.

RACIAL INEQUITIES

A Pew Research Center survey of 6,637 from January 22 to February 5, 2019, revealed large gaps in the life experiences of people living in the US. Sixty-five percent of Black Americans reported that "people acted like they were suspicious of them based on their race or ethnicity." Sixty percent reported that people acted like they thought they were not smart. Only 26 percent of White Americans reported that happening in their lifetime.

In the same survey, 61 percent of Black Americans reported being subjected to racial slurs and jokes and 43 percent feared for their personal safety because of their race or ethnicity. When taken together, these numbers demonstrate that the majority of Black Americans have experienced some form of trauma related to the color of their skin.

The data in schools indicates that trauma doesn't stop at the front gate. Gaps in academic achievement, suspension rates, drop-out rates, and funding tell a story of a system that struggles to meet the needs of all students.

ADVERSE CHILDHOOD EXPERIENCES

Adverse Childhood Experiences, or ACEs, are events that cause toxic levels of stress hormones that can interrupt normal physical and mental development. Students that are subjected to ACEs are more likely to struggle in school and suffer with emotional and behavioral challenges. A child who appears to be defiant in the classroom could actually be a child who is working on surviving their childhood with the tools they have.

ACEs are linked to lower educational attainment, unemployment, poverty, alcoholism, drug abuse, depression, suicide, poor physical health, and obesity—not just for young people but throughout their lives.

ACEs events include abuse, neglect, watching a family member experience violence, substance misuse or mental illness in the household, parental separation or divorce, and an incarcerated household member. The Centers for Disease Control and Prevention (CDC), in partnership with Kaiser Permanente, conducted a landmark ACE study from 1995 to 1997 with more than 17,000 participants. The study found that almost 40 percent of a 17,000 person sample reported two or more adverse childhood experiences and 12.5 percent experienced four or more.

The great news for students is that their local school can be part of their healing. Current ACEs research indicates that supportive adult relationships can mitigate much of the potential impact of these traumatizing events.

POLITICAL POLARIZATION

A Pew Research Center report on a survey of 10,000 adults nationwide remarked that, "Republicans and Democrats are more divided along ideological lines—and partisan antipathy is deeper and more extensive—than at any point in the last two decades." That was in 2014.

The 2020 election and COVID-19 didn't make the polarization any smaller. On top of dealing with changing federal guidance, local school officials also dealt with diminishing trust in government in general, including educational leaders.

MOVING FORWARD

There is hope even in the midst of all of these challenges. Schools and districts across the country have demonstrated that when they are able to bring their school community together with a student-centered approach, they can tackle some of the thorniest issues in society.

The key is effective communication. That starts with doing enough research to truly understand how the issues affect your school. It is also about doing the work to understand your community—where are they on these issues? Where is the common ground? What are the values everyone can agree on? What do you all want for students?

Be open to new solutions that emerge as a result of research and open, two-way communication. They may not be the same ones you started with or imagined, but a diversity of opinions can lead you to even better ones.

Create systems that support your effective communication so that it ceases to be an additional burden and instead becomes part of your leadership culture—a non-negotiable expectation.

BRANDING

As you were deciding about whether or not to pick up this book, you might have wondered why a school administrator needs to know any of this communication stuff. Why do we need to sell our schools? Can't we just come to campus, do a great job educating students, and count on our good work to tell our story?

The answer to that is complicated. While the most essential thing a school can do is a great job with the core mission of growing young minds, there is a lot more to leading a school than there used to be. For example, for decades, almost all students in the United States attended the school down the road from them without any consideration of a potentially "better" option out there.

Today, students and families have choices. There is unprecedented competition in the educational world. Charter schools, private schools, homeschooling, and online schools each offer a unique proposition to potential students. They may have specialized programs, offer the opportunity to get out of an undesirable neighborhood, or even offer direct payments to families to purchase curriculum and technology for their home.

In addition, schools are under unprecedented scrutiny. With a quick online search, families can pull up comparative test scores, online rating sites, social media commentary and media stories that follow a campus for decades. There is no way to control the fact that people will search out this information—however, a savvy school leader will be able to ensure that much of what people see is positive. That online presence is one aspect of a school's brand.

In addition, there is increased competition to hire the best teachers. With shortages in much of the country, recently certificated educators will be doing their research about where they want to work, comparing schools and districts.

WHAT IS A BRAND?

Thinking about a brand may conjure the swoosh of Nike, the brown trucks of United Parcel Service, or the Clydesdale Super Bowl commercials of Budweiser. An active social media user may think about the smart and snarky wit of the Wendy's and Merriam-Webster Dictionary Twitter accounts. These are elements of branding, but branding also includes the return policy of luxury retailer Nordstrom and the happy atmosphere at Disneyland, as well as the cranky attitudes and long lines you might encounter at your local department of motor vehicles.

In short, a brand is the full experience of the organization—the look, feel, vibe, and internal spirit of the place. You don't need a brochure to tell you that the employees at Southwest who sing the safety rules are enjoying their job and are respected by leadership in the company. The experience of watching them smile, joke, and tease each other is far more impactful than a marketing commercial might be.

The same is true at schools. If the people that come to visit a campus feel welcome, if they engage positively with the school secretary and see smiling students connecting with each other and staff, they will know a lot about whether or not they want to look into the school further. The reverse is true if their experience is less than ideal.

A brand isn't just about the experiences of students, families, and community members, but also of the staff who work at a campus. Do they feel respected and listened to? Do they feel connected to the school and its mission, vision, and values? Bringing employees into decision-making and increasing trust and connections through the methods described in chapter 11 and chapter 12 on internal communication and culture building, respectively, can help. Once they are feeling committed to the school, team members can become valued partners in promoting campus strengths and increasing the perception of the brand.

WHAT PARENTS WANT

When beginning the process of understanding and developing a campus brand, it helps to start with understanding the educational marketplace. What is it that parents in your neighborhood are most looking for in a school?

There are some basics that all families are looking for, like a safe and clean campus with friendly front office staff and caring, qualified teachers. Beyond the foundational elements, doing some research with families provides leaders with guidance about which among their strengths they should emphasize in messaging, as well as what they may try to develop if it doesn't already exist. For example, if families are looking for a strong math, science, and engineering pathway; additional courses and enrichment programs can be added in that area.

Some of the most commonly listed priorities families have listed include academic rigor, test scores, arts and music programs, and technology equipment. Small class sizes, academic and athletic achievement, and involved parents also generally rank highly. However, to ensure that a school's messaging is targeted, chapters 1 and 2 on research techniques can assist leaders in their efforts to narrow the list.

SELL YOUR STRENGTHS

While every school has a unique blend of strengths and assets, some of the most successful campuses document high levels of community and parent involvement, flourishing alumni programs, and high demand for enrollment and employment.

Each leader likely has some idea of the strengths of their campus, but it can be enlightening to ask a variety of people associated with the school about their perception. For example, are there special programs that have a strong reputation and attract families?

What kind of before and after school childcare is available? What kinds of enrichment programs, clubs, and activities are offered? All of these have the potential to attract students and families.

Take a look at the competition in your area and focus on those strengths that only your school can boast about. If your competition is a small private school, the strongest messaging might be to highlight the wide variety of classes, athletic teams, and special clubs available—something families would not likely find in the competition.

Once the best messaging is identified, ensure that it is communicated as often as possible. People remember messages through repetition and simplicity. Developing supportive communication systems like those in chapter 8 make it easier to ensure people are exposed to those messages in a variety of ways. Some quick and inexpensive ways to spread simple, positive messages include staff email signature lines, the bottom of meeting agendas, voicemail and call waiting messages, memo pads, and business cards. The genius of these methods is that these passive tools keep communicating key messages without active involvement.

The chapters in the implementing section of this book (chapters 7–14) provide a variety of ideas for communicating inside and outside the school building, from customer service to internal communication and social media. The most important common element is the consistency and commitment across methods.

Remember that one communication method alone will not sufficiently build a brand because it is about the complete customer experience. Satisfied staff, families, and community members who speak positively about your school are the most effective tool possible. Regardless of your message, theme, or slogan, no marketing effort can be effective without the support of those most connected to the campus.

The communication practices in this book will help you understand the strengths of your campus and how they overlap with the desires of your community. They will help you develop key messages, plan for success, and implement campaigns that ensure your students, staff, families, and community are connected to your school and support your vision for the future.

Part I

Research

TWO

Research as a Foundation

New elementary school principal Marissa Alexander sighed deeply as she analyzed the data from last weekend's parent survey. Once again, the low percentage of responses from her school's Spanish-speaking families was significant and a cause for growing concern. Were they receiving the correspondence? Was their contact information up to date?

She was confident that every communication she sent out had been translated from English to Spanish via Google Translate but rather than speculate or waste time, she decided to conduct her own research. She began by reaching out to Spanish teacher Mrs. Rodriguez to ask for help with translating as she made direct calls to the families. In call after call, as Principal Alexander took copious notes of their responses, the reason for the families' lack of responsiveness became glaringly obvious—they couldn't understand the messages!

After collecting data from the parents, Principal Alexander continued to do online research looking up possible barriers to effective translation. She learned there were many hindrances for her Spanish-speaking families. In many cases, Google Translate is limited in its ability to properly translate words or phrases with multiple meanings. However, the most common complaint she found was related to regional dialect. With more than 65 languages used in Mexico resulting in 350 dialects, Google Translate could only recognize a few of them. So, while parents could understand parts of certain messages, overall they were confused by the sentence structure. As a result, families with different dialects began to feel alienated and disengaged.

Buoyed by the findings of her research, Principal Alexander set about to solve the communication issue experienced by her Spanish-speaking families. Her first plan of action was to limit her use of online translation services and utilize her Spanish teachers to review and translate her notices, letters, and surveys from the school. Next, she would create an advisory committee of Spanish-speaking

11

parents/volunteers to help ensure proper messaging, from vocabulary to tone, was being used when communicating with Spanish-speaking families.

When the topic of research comes up, it seems that school leaders seem to think the area is reserved for the folks in lab coats or statisticians in front of computer screens. The truth is, our schools are conducting research nearly every day—we just need to take notice and document what we learn.

There are a number of research myths that tend to get in the way of people believing they can conduct research on behalf of their school or district. Many people believe it has to be expensive or conducted by an outside company. Not true. There are many examples of research done with very little funding aside from staff time that provided a great deal of helpful information.

Another myth is that each time an issue comes up, there needs to be a new effort to conduct a unique research process. Not true. Research doesn't have to be done specifically for your topic. Many times, adding a question or two into an already planned survey can yield plenty of information.

While it doesn't require a lot of extra time or money, getting quality results from your research does require some creativity and some curiosity about bias. For example, online surveys are wonderful for collecting a lot of information quickly, but if a significant portion of families do not have easy access to the internet or they speak a different language, it takes some creativity to reach them and some understanding of how the results may be skewed based on the survey methodology.

To understand how to be creative with research ideas, it helps to have some basic knowledge about the types of communication research available. There are four general perspectives: primary/secondary, qualitative/quantitative, formal/informal, and formative/evaluative. Most research techniques can be classified using these perspectives that are outlined in table 2.1 which also provides examples of school-based research ideas.

PRIMARY VS SECONDARY

Who collected the information is the most important question to ask to decide if the research is primary or secondary. If you or your organization collected the information, the research can be classified as "primary." A survey of your families or staff, the count of the number of people who called about a specific concern, or interviews you conduct with subject matter experts would all qualify as primary research.

If someone else collected the information, that makes the research secondary, though no less useful. State or federally provided data on

Table 2.1.

Question: Who collected the information?

Primary	Secondary
• Survey of your families or staff • # of people who called about a specific concern • Interviews with subject matter experts	• State or federal data on education issues • City or neighborhood demographic information • Regional academic data

Question: Words or numbers?

Qualitative	Quantitative
• Focus groups • Open-ended questions on surveys • Observing behavior	• Multiple choice, rating, or true/false questions on surveys • Counting the number of people who attend an event • Enrollment numbers at a school or in a program

Questions: Can it be replicated and is it random?

Formal(ish)	Informal
• Automated phone system survey • Online survey (as long as the entire population has access or survey is also provided in print) • Documenting positive, neutral, and negative press coverage based on preestablished protocol	• Interviews with key influencers • Focus groups to test messages or strategies • Group meetings allowing public feedback

Question: How will it be used?

Formative	Evaluative
• Baseline survey of audience awareness, attitude, or behavior • Feedback on initial messaging and strategies • Documenting historical enrollment trends	• Post-campaign survey of audience awareness, attitude, or behavior • Measuring growth of enrollment after a campaign • Measuring growth in event attendance over the year before

---

education issues, city or neighborhood demographic information, and regional academic data are all examples of helpful secondary research.

QUALITATIVE VS QUANTITATIVE

This is likely the easiest category for most people to identify. When the research involves studying something that is difficult to quantify, like first-person descriptions that are unique to the individual, it is likely qualitative. Focus groups, open-ended questions on surveys, and observing behavior at parent pick-up are all examples of qualitative research.

If you are able to easily quantify what you are researching, it is a different story. Multiple choice and rating or true/false questions on surveys are prime examples of quantitative research. So are other numbers-based processes, like counting how many people attend an event or looking at enrollment numbers at a school or in a program.

In short, if you want to understand the nature of something, qualitative methods can provide answers, if you want to understand the scope of an issue, that's likely quantitative territory.

FORMAL VS INFORMAL

There are two essential questions related to classifying research as formal or informal—is it random and can it be replicated? Random means that there is equal probability that anyone could have had a chance to participate, increasing the likelihood that the results represent a larger population. If it can be replicated and the results are highly likely to turn out the same each time, that's another basic characteristic of formal research.

Automated phone system surveys can qualify as formal research, as long as the time of the call doesn't unintentionally bias the type of person who might respond. For example, if a live phone survey is conducted during the day, people who work are likely to be underrepresented in the results.

Online surveys can also qualify as formal as long as the entire population has internet access or if the survey is also provided in print form. Even something that seems as subjective as documenting positive, neutral, and negative press coverage can be elevated to the level of formal research if the classification of positive, neutral, and negative is based on preestablished protocol or a set of guidelines that has been tested reliably with several classifiers who continue to come up with the same results.

Anecdotal information or feedback that is gathered by convenience is informal research. Interviews with an audience's key influencers, focus groups to test messages or strategies, or the comments gathered at group meetings allowing public feedback are all types of informal research. While informal research results cannot be applied as representative of larger groups, informal data can be very useful supplementary information, helping to understand the exact nature of something hinted at in formal data.

FORMATIVE VS EVALUATIVE

Formative and evaluative research is easy to classify based on the function of the data. Will it help a school principal decide what to do to communicate or will it help her understand whether it's been done successfully?

Formative research is the kind of research that helps to discover more information about an issue or preview messaging or tools before they are used on a larger scale. Conducting a baseline survey of audience awareness, attitude, or behavior to benchmark where a campaign started is also a great formative research tool that should be used more often. Collecting feedback on initial messaging and strategies and documenting historical enrollment trends to predict what type of campaign will be needed are additional examples of formative research.

Evaluative research comes into play as a measurement of what a communication effort has accomplished against the objectives that were set in the plan. A post-campaign survey of audience awareness, attitude, or behavior to measure growth is evaluative in nature. Measuring the growth of student enrollment after a campaign or measuring growth in event attendance over the previous year are also evaluative research tools.

Understanding the types and examples of research available can demystify what it means to be data-driven in our approach. Once people begin to review the everyday examples of research tools that can be put to work in campaigns, the task of being well informed about the issue and audiences and acting with intention when selecting communication methods becomes a simpler and more common approach to every communication situation.

Research doesn't have to be complicated, table 2.2 provides additional samples of things you may already have done—but perhaps didn't call "research."

SURVEYS

The elephant in the room when it comes to surveys is this: don't ask if you don't plan to do anything with the results. Surveys are work for everyone involved. They have to be designed, written, put into the correct platform, tested, revised, distributed, and marketed. The results have to be tallied, analyzed, and interpreted for action. Respondents invest time taking the survey as well. Before anyone decides to conduct a survey, they must first decide if they really want input.

If the results come back and they don't align with the expectation or direction the school was planning to take, what will happen? Is this a sincere effort to collect guidance and feedback from stakeholders or a show of engagement to check a box or appease a certain group? The worst thing a school can do is ask for opinions and not use them. Respect the time of everyone involved and only use a survey *if* the feedback will matter.

Table 2.2.

Source	Data
Town hall meeting	# participants, #comments, pro/con/neutral rating of comments, qualitative input
Referendum results	Voter participation rates, pockets of support/non-support, voter demographics
Enrollment	Geographic mapping of student addresses, numbers up or down over previous years, comparisons to other schools/districts, demographic snapshot of current families, demographic trends
Social media engagement	likes, comments, retweets, followers gained or lost
Transfer form	Reason for transfer (open field or multiple choice), neighborhood (from address), home school, transfer school
Parent-teacher conferences	Live survey responses, attendance rates by school, grade, demographics
Media monitoring	# releases or announcements picked up, positive v negative or neutral coverage type, success rates with various outlets, ratio of stories sent to published/aired
Surprise shopper	Data on predetermined rubric instrument, additional observations not captured by rubric
Census	# families, # children under 18, demographics
District app downloads	# downloads, by school, by grade
Interview with leader or influencer	Information on topic, additional leaders or influencers to talk to, communication tool ideas
Chamber of Commerce perception survey	Awareness of programs, perception/satisfaction with schools, suggestions for programs and communication tools
Internal communication and morale survey	Ratings of communication and morale, survey participation rates by role, location

QUESTIONS TO ASK BEFORE YOU SURVEY

After the biggest question is out of the way, there are a few more that will help shape the development of a survey. What is the purpose? What is the school leadership trying to learn or understand? Is it a survey to tease out overall perceptions of the campus, determine support for a program, or discover communication preferences? Will it help establish a baseline so that a change in perception, awareness, or self-reported behavior can be measured in the future after a communication effort?

Next, what will a parent, student or community member receive from completing the survey? What's their stake in helping the school or district? This important question will help guide the marketing of the survey. Is there a way to tie the benefit of the survey back to students and families? Perhaps the results will guide decision-making on an issue, provide insight about the features wanted in a new school or program, or help the school or district better communicate, strengthening families' capacity to support student learning. Get to the benefit of the respondents and communicate it widely when you are promoting the survey.

When and how are respondents likely to engage in the survey and what devices, if any, are they likely to use? Popular survey methodologies include online (via a computer, tablet, or smartphone to a survey portal), telephone (via automated dialing responses to a voice prompt or speaking with a live surveyor), and in-person responding to questions from a live surveyor. Analytics of previous surveys, if available, can provide insights into preferred options. If the data shows a significant population lacks access to the internet, maybe an online survey is not the best tool for the job. If English is a second language for a significant segment of the population being surveyed, ensuring the survey is available in other languages is essential. It goes without saying—available resources including funds for the required technology or live surveyors will need to be factored into the decision.

Also consider the last time that a survey was sent out to the same audience. If you've created a centralized list of surveys, you'll have that information at your fingertips. It's important to not over-survey your stakeholders. Reserve the request for the times you truly need input to make a good decision or plan to move forward. Consider if a full survey is needed or questions can be added to one that is already scheduled.

It's also important to find as "neutral" a time as possible—for example, not when teachers are pressured at the end of quarters or semesters to get in grades, not when it's standardized testing time, not when there are lots of other activities that involve parents such as the start of school or end of school year, and so forth. Be prepared to move your survey if a crisis hits just prior.

SURVEY DESIGN AND DEVELOPMENT

Once the decisions around purpose, methodology, and schedule are determined, it is time to outline the survey. Based on the type of feedback the school needs to collect through the effort, develop an outline with a general phrase to represent each question or section of questions, not worrying about the specific wording yet. The outline helps with ordering the questions in a way that makes sense for the respondents. For example, group questions about a similar topic together and start with foundational or general questions before moving to more specific questions.

When the outline is complete, it is time to craft the wording. In the introduction, aim to be transparent with the audience about the purpose of the study, including language in marketing messages. The purpose might include how the input will be used, and what changes are likely to be made from the feedback. When possible, tie the effort back to how it will impact students and student learning. If the survey is anonymous, let respondents know up front. Anonymous surveys are more likely to receive honest critical feedback if respondents are confident that they won't be identified through their answers.

After the introduction and overview, consider the demographic information you wish to collect on the respondents. Knowing how you will want to analyze the results by different segments of your survey population will help guide these decisions. Will you want to know the respondent's connection to the school or district? Another might be the length of relationship with the school or district or how they heard about the survey. Table 2.3 is an example of the categories to consider including in a question about respondent's role in the district.

The more categories that are included, the more specific the analysis of the data can be. For example, using cross tabulation, usually an easy automatic function of most online survey tools, the responses to questions on the rest of the survey can be separated by the answer to the role question. How district administrators answered a question can be compared to how teachers answered the same question. One note of caution on demographic questions: if the survey is anonymous, give consideration to questions that may compromise that anonymity. For example, if you ask respondents to identify the school in which they work and also ask them to identify their job title, a principal or school secretary or music teacher most likely knows that they are the only one in that role in their school, making their answers easy to connect back to them as individuals.

Throughout the development of the survey, pay special attention to the specific wording. Keep the language as simple as possible, creating a conversational tone and avoiding educational jargon. If the survey is be-

---

Table 2.3.

Please select the option below that best represents your role with ABC School District.

    a. Parent or family member of a student
    b. Student
    c. Community member, not a parent or staff member
    d. Teacher
    e. Site support
    f. Site administrator
    g. District support
    h. District administrator

ing written in Microsoft Word, one of the proofing options is to show readability statistics. The same option is available in Google Docs. The readability score will provide an initial idea about how accessible the survey will be for respondents.

Cultural considerations are also important when it comes to wording. For example, one of the changes that has been made in a lot of schools and districts is the reference to the adult responsible for a student. In the past, that word has usually been "parent." However, a number of social and demographic changes have increased the number of households in which someone other than a parent is the adult schools and districts are communicating with. Instead, many schools and districts are now using the terms families or family members to ensure all households are represented.

In addition to wording, questions with rating scales should remain consistent throughout the survey and generally helpful to have the lowest mark on the left and the highest on the right, although the research on the topic doesn't indicate an impact on results. Table 2.4 provides an example of a question with a Likert scale response that meets these guidelines.

If it is a multiple choice question, be sure that all the possible response categories are offered or include "other" as an option so that every respondent sees an answer that reflects their experience.

In addition to the wording and the format of each individual question, the length of the survey needs to be considered. How long will it take to complete? As a general rule, five minutes or less is recommended. On occasion, a longer survey might be needed. In either case, it's a good idea to let the respondents know how long they should expect to spend on the survey. A "progress bar" at the top of each page also helps them gauge the experience.

Once the initial draft is complete, select the most appropriate survey tool and send a test version out to a small sample of respondents. Talk with the sample respondents about the purpose of each question and whether they interpreted them in the way they were intended. Rework the questions that are confusing for respondents.

Table 2.4.

Please rate your agreement with the following statements on a scale of 1–5. 1 (Strongly disagree) 2(Disagree) 3(Neutral) 4(Agree) 5(Strongly agree)	
My child's school is a welcoming place for parents.	1 2 3 4 5
My child's teacher appreciates parent volunteers in the classroom.	1 2 3 4 5
I feel like my opinion is valued by my child's school staff.	1 2 3 4 5

When the survey has been pre-tested and the wording is finalized, it's time to send it out. If it is a survey by invitation, it should be sent to a representative sample of the full audience universe. With a sample, you need to get a much higher percentage of people responding than when going with the full universe to get the same margin of error.

Like any other communication effort, develop a plan for how to reach potential respondents. If it is an internal survey for employees, the outreach is simple and can be accomplished through email invitations and department announcements. If a school or district has email addresses for all families, a similar approach may work. If not, the school or district should review the audiences that need to be reached and the communication tools available, developing a plan for getting the survey invitation out as many ways as possible. A survey outreach plan template is available in the supplemental materials at www.schoolprpro.com/the-communicating-principal.

SURVEY DISTRIBUTION

As a general rule, two weeks is a good period of time for a survey to be open. Any longer than that and people may feel they have plenty of time to respond and forget. Shorter than that may not leave enough time for maximum responses. Try to avoid holidays or breaks as part of the two-week period if possible. Keep in mind, though, that an extension of the survey period that does not present conflict could result in a higher response rate and may be worthwhile to the cause.

The outreach plan should include an initial invitation and at least one reminder on the day before the survey ends. Depending on the audience and the number of communication tools, a midpoint reminder might be a good option, but if there are a number of tools being utilized, it could be over the top. Some districts have found multiple reminders to yield good results, so it is a decision that will be based on your unique circumstances and audiences. In either case, the reminders can and should be delivered in different ways and at different times of the day and week.

It's the content that drives participation rates in many district surveys. On a recent mental health survey of staff, a school district realized a 90 percent response rate. The communication director explained that anything that helps staff impact students in a positive way or that helps them monitor student achievement and well-being is always a top interest area for respondents. In the outreach plan, it should be easy to communicate how the survey will benefit students.

Once the overall outreach plan is developed, think through the survey outreach messaging as thoroughly as the survey wording. Keep it short, conversational, and again use simple wording. Remember to include the language around the purpose for the survey and how the information will support student and student learning. It may be helpful to include a sample question that is easy to answer. For example, in a survey about communication preferences, try something like: "How are you reading this? We want to know! Help ABC school get even better at communicating with our families!" Develop tool-specific messages, longer for media articles and websites, shorter for Facebook and Twitter. Given the right amount of time and effective messaging, the responses should roll in.

When a survey is open to any respondent to opt in, be mindful of the potential for voluntary response bias. This occurs when results are composed largely of respondents having strong opinions on one side or another of an issue. The resulting responses tend to overrepresent people who have strong opinions on one side or another of an issue. There may not be anything that can be done to avoid this kind of bias, it just needs to be accounted for when interpreting the results. For example, on a survey of changing school start times, it may appear that families are polarized into two camps, very much in support of the change or very against the change. When compared against the total number of possible respondents however, it becomes obvious the great majority doesn't have an opinion about the topic. Attaining a large enough percentage of respondents that translates to a low margin of error can help overcome voluntary response bias.

Incentives offer another area of consideration. Contests in which responses are entered for prizes can sometimes increase the number of people who participate in a survey, but may compromise the quality of responses. If people are able to submit multiple responses to win a prize, it may taint the representativeness of the population as a whole.

Lastly, the survey responses need to be reviewed not just for the content, but also for representation in significant segments of the survey population. If a particular segment is not participating, do some digging to find out why. Did they not hear about the survey through the communication tools that were used? Did they feel that their voice wouldn't be heard so they didn't want to waste their time? A small focus group may lead to some great insights about gaps in trust or communication methods.

Analysis and interpretation may seem like the final step in a survey, but there are two more. What will change as a result of the input? What decisions will be affected? How will the information guide future programs and communication efforts? These questions need to be both asked and answered. The "so what" of the results needs to be identified and translated into a focused explanation of what was learned. "Here is what we learned, and here is what we plan to do about it." The "so what" can then be utilized as post messaging for the survey and turned into visuals and graphics that make it easy to understand what the results mean. There is a lot more discussion of the reporting of data in chapter 16.

Lastly, in addition to telling audiences what you learned, do not forget to thank them for their time and input. Use the same outreach plan you used with your participation campaign to let them know that you listened and the time they spent on the survey is valued. List the numbers that participated, key insights, and how those insights will be applied to make the school better at serving students and families. This may impact both the likelihood that they will participate the next time as well as their respect and support for the school or district. We all like to be heard even when a decision doesn't go our way. At the very least, we like to know the time and energy we invested in something mattered. Table 2.5 provides a list of tips for creating, formatting, and distributing a survey.

It may all seem overwhelming at first, especially if the school is new at asking for guidance and feedback. The most important thing is to keep asking. You may not learn all that you expect with your first survey, but you will learn something, even if it is how to do better with the next one.

Table 2.5.

Top 20 List of General Survey Tips

1. Don't ask if the results won't change anything.
2. Know your purpose and communicate it to respondents.
3. Know what's in it for respondents and communicate it.
4. Design the survey for the way it will be taken—laptop, phone, paper, verbal.
5. Don't over-survey, use information from other efforts when possible.
6. Create an outline before you attempt question wording.
7. Order survey questions by topic area.
8. If you say the survey will be anonymous, ensure it will be.
9. Use simple language in descriptive text and questions, avoid educational jargon.
10. Consider cultural differences in terms of the wording and distribution.
11. Rating scales should be consistent.
12. Keep the survey to less than 5 minutes.
13. Pretest and revise.
14. Let respondents know how long it will take and where they are in the survey.
15. Create a communications plan for the survey distribution.
16. Keep it open for about two weeks, avoid holidays and breaks.
17. Be thoughtful in creating survey outreach messaging.
18. Consider possible bias impacts in analyzing results.
19. Clearly define and articulate the "so what" of the results.
20. Reuse your outreach plan to tell people you listened and what will change.

ASK & ANSWER

- What do you hope to learn with your research?
- Are you willing to make adjustments based on what you learn from the research?
- What research have other organizations/schools already completed that can help with your communication goals?

Supplemental training materials available for this chapter at www.schoolprpro.com/the-communicating-principal.

THREE

Qualitative Research

High school principal Katrina Maxwell was facing mounting pressure from senior high school students, staff, and families to announce plans for the Class of 2020 senior prom. The Stay-at-Home Order issued by the governor as a result of the COVID-19 pandemic had closed schools indefinitely and disrupted traditional senior activities and events. About one month after the order, unnerved parents and melancholy seniors were increasingly anxious to hear from her about what to expect.

Like thousands of high school principals throughout the nation, the question before Principal Maxwell was, how do you reimagine a senior prom that honors the tradition while ensuring the health and safety of students and staff?

Looking to quickly collect stakeholder opinions on the matter, Principal Maxwell convened an online meeting with her team and decided to create a survey for all high school parents, students, and staff. The purpose of the eight-question survey was to collect feedback regarding how the senior prom would be celebrated. Created in Google Forms, the document asked questions like, "What ideas do you have to celebrate our seniors as an alternative to prom?" and "What do you think about a virtual prom?"

Respondents were also asked to identify their stakeholder group and given one week to respond. As the surveys began to pour in, Principal Maxwell was surprised by the spectrum of responses. Many staff members (who also serve as senior class sponsors) indicated they wanted the event to be held virtually, while a significant number of students and parents outright rejected the idea.

A closer look at the responses revealed that the disunity about how to proceed stemmed from a fundamental rift between each group's interpretation of social distancing guidelines. Some students advocating postponement, not cancellation, of the physical prom maintained the view that social distancing guidelines would be lifted after April 2020. Many of those opinions cited information from the Institute for Health Metrics and Evaluation (IHME), an independent global health research organization founded by Bill and Melinda Gates.

Teachers and staff, while wanting to do their best to salvage their students' senior year memories, relied heavily on information from the State Board of Education (who warned that social distancing would go well into the start of the 2020–2021 school year). Underclassmen who were not directly impacted also took the survey and speculated about their future senior proms.

Despite her best effort to quickly gather feedback from her school community, Principal Maxwell was unable to extract any common theme from her survey. While the qualitative data did not offer enough quantitative data to make a decision, the survey was helpful in understanding why people felt the way they did. Formative research can greatly assist school leaders with gauging their stakeholders' attitudes or awareness of an issue. It also allows leaders to guide people in the desired direction for consensus.

Qualitative research sometimes doesn't get the respect it deserves. It is messy, it doesn't provide black and white solutions, and it doesn't easily translate into a statistical report that makes people feel heard. However, it can provide insights that would never be uncovered by a simple multiple-choice survey. If you are interested in the scope of the problem, use quantitative research; but if the interest is the nature of the problem, use qualitative research.

While many of these qualitative research methods might not be able to provide high-confidence generalizations about populations, they all can provide unique value under the right circumstances. Qualitative methods provide a richness in understanding that is impossible to get from quantitative methods alone. Qualitative methods give us the words and phrases that our audiences are using, and sometimes bring up questions we might not think to ask. This is especially important when you and your staff don't have a lot in common with the students, families, or other stakeholders that you are reaching out to.

With qualitative methods, the researcher has to let go of a certain amount of control and follow where the experience leads. While in most cases there are replicable data collection procedures (like checklists, questionnaires, and facilitator guides), the researcher has to be comfortable with *exploring* the topic rather than *confirming* their thinking and anything they believe they know about the topic. Letting go can be uncomfortable for some people but it is an excellent source of real-life, respondent-driven feedback.

The key to obtaining the best qualitative research is choosing the right method and the right tools. Just like developing an effective four-step PR plan, school leaders need to be sensitive to the problem, the multiple audiences, the best applicable research method, and how the questions and tools may need to be tailored differently for each audience. Let's review some of the qualitative methods available for examining different issues in school communications. Table 3.1 includes a description of a variety of methods and examples of each.

DIRECT OBSERVATION

There are a number of valuable qualitative methods that can easily be undertaken. One is simply direct observation, and it is likely something you are already doing without calling it research. As an example, did you receive a complaint about the way that students are behaving in front of the campus after school each day? Park across the street for a few days as school gets out and observe the activity for patterns. To formalize it, create a checklist to use while observing and mark on the list what happens—while the observational approach is qualitative in nature, adding up the observed behavior on the checklist turns it into quantitative data that can reinforce how generalizable the observations are. It only hap-

Table 3.1.

Method	Description	Examples
Direct Observation	Watching activity or touring an area and taking notes about what is happening	Observing student behavior in front of campus, observing pick up and drop off, secret shopper
Interview	Sitting down with a subject matter expert, impacted audience, or influencer	Talking with a parent who transferred out of district, talking with a school leader who has experienced a similar issue
Case Study	Intense study of a specific person or example	Developing a description of how a crisis was handled in a neighboring district, developing a description of how one student changed their academic circumstances through hard work
Focus Group	Bringing representatives of a group together to discuss a particular topic or preview messages	Group of students come together to discuss new dress code policy, group of teachers come together to discuss restorative justice
Open-Ended Question	Questions requiring a text answer on a survey	Anything else you would like to tell us?
Advisory Group	Ongoing informal gathering of people willing to provide helpful critical feedback	Curriculum and instruction group, communication and PR group

pened once? Maybe it is not that big of a challenge. If a problem behavior is documented multiple times, that's something to look into further.

Is there a specific area that could use an after-school staff assignment? Were the students well-behaved? Maybe the concerned caller caught the school on a bad day or misinterpreted what they saw. Either way, observing what is happening will provide the answers.

INTERVIEW

Another qualitative option that can be very helpful is an interview with someone impacted by the issue or perhaps a subject matter expert in the area. It's a good idea to start with an initial set of questions on the topic, but be sure to leave room for unstructured discussion. A question like, "Is there anything else about this I should know?" or "Is there anything else you want to share?" can bring out a lot of valuable information. The use of open-ended questions leads to much richer conversation and deeper understanding than closed-ended questions. The interviewee is free to move the conversation in any direction and the discoveries can be surprising. While the school or district leader may think a particular issue is about one thing like budget cuts, some stakeholder groups may think it is about something else, like respect for teacher input.

Interviewing other school leaders that have been through an experience or conducted a campaign similar to the one you are considering is another great example of qualitative research. There is no reason to re-create the wheel when undertaking a new campaign. In most cases, there are many other schools and districts that have implemented communication campaigns that can provide valuable lessons learned or even specific strategies and tactics.

CASE STUDIES

A case study is an intensive study of a specific individual or specific context. It examines specific samples to better understand a phenomenon that occurs more broadly. Case studies are often used as a follow-up when school or district leaders find themes reflected in quantitative data that they want to better understand.

For example, one district discovered that one of the biggest dips in enrollment was occurring between sixth and seventh grade when students moved from the elementary campus to the junior high school. A district administrator reached out to one of the families that left the district the year before and developed a case study on their experience which shed light on a number of issues at the elementary and junior high The case study was shared with principals at all district schools as an example of the importance of customer service and building positive perceptions of district schools. One of the downsides of a case study is that some of the people who may need to learn the lessons from it will think it is limited in scope and doesn't apply to them. However, when presented in conjunction with representative quantitative data, it can be very powerful.

FOCUS GROUPS

One of the qualitative methods that are generally well understood by most people is focus groups. Fundamentally, they are group interviews usually with people who have a common experience, like they may all be preschool teachers. The interviews can be as informal as inviting some students into a room with some snacks to talk about an issue and as formal as hosting a group at a testing facility with one-way glass that allows researchers to watch the group underway. They can be used as formative research while strategies and messages are being developed, as a pretest when strategies and messaging are ready to be launched and as an evaluative method after a campaign to determine the impact it had and even the perception of the campaign itself.

Some simple guidelines will ensure that focus groups are as effective as possible. The list of questions for the group should be developed and reviewed ahead of time to ensure they will get at the information that is needed. Pre-testing the list of questions with someone who is similar to the focus group participants can be very helpful. Like developing a good survey, it's important to avoid unnecessary jargon and not to be too prescriptive. The more open the questions are, the more unexpected and potentially meaningful the feedback might be.

During the group session, the facilitator should ensure that no one member is dominating the discussion or making it uncomfortable for others to participate in the discussion. Creating a comfortable atmosphere is essential to getting good input. To that end, the first few questions on the list should be easy warm-ups, avoiding topics that might be polarizing until later in the session. It might be helpful to have one person facilitate the focus group questions and another person take notes during the conversations.

It is also a good idea to have multiple focus groups to be able to compare reactions and elicit the range of possible responses (feelings, perceptions, knowledge, attitudes) to the questions or messages. Getting people to participate in groups can be challenging—consider offering childcare, refreshments, and stipends to make it more attractive to prospective participants.

OPEN-ENDED QUESTIONS

When school leaders opt to include open-ended questions on a survey that is mostly quantitative, it adds more work to the survey analysis but also provides the opportunity to learn something outside of what was expected. Some examples of open-ended questions include:

- Are there any other thoughts you want to share about our district?
- Is there any other communication tool we should be using to reach you?
- What is the best thing about your child's school?
- Do you have any suggestions for our administrative team?
- What else do you need to know about this issue that has not been mentioned here?

Asking open-ended questions is not for the faint of heart. There might be some difficult or even mean-spirited feedback, there may also be some nonsensical or nonresponsive content. However, there will likely also be important gems that reveal information that would never have been discovered in a multiple-choice question.

Analysis of open-ended questions can be time-consuming. It involves collecting all the feedback and organizing it by theme and also taking note of how often the same comment was made to ascertain how representative the content might be.

Sometimes qualitative research isn't even a conscious, formalized research effort, but rather just a smart way to become informed. For example, it is usually a good idea to seek out diverse viewpoints, particularly on a polarizing issue. Many school leaders make a habit of developing a group of "critical friends" that they meet with regularly to preview ideas and help anticipate potential challenges.

Qualitative methods complement quantitative research. When conducted first, qualitative methods help us determine the questions to ask in a quantitative way to find out if what we learned on a small scale applies to the population at large. After a quantitative effort, qualitative research can also draw out details that are impossible to explore in other ways. In fact, the two types of research together may be the best recipe for effective data-driven decision-making.

ASK & ANSWER

- How will you use the data after it's collected and analyzed to assure your stakeholders you heard them?
- Do you have a diverse team that can assist you with properly interpreting responses from your community?

- Do your research questions challenge your own assumptions about an issue?

Supplemental training materials available for this chapter at www.schoolprpro.com/the-communicating-principal.

Part II

Planning

FOUR

Understanding Your Audiences

Duluth High School principal Jeff Hubert had worked for months with his district's director of safety on the hiring of the district's first-ever School Resource Officer (SRO). The rise of school shootings, bullying, and an overall national focus on school safety were central to the school board's decision to hire local police officer James Bensen for the new position. Principal Hubert was excited to begin his campaign to share the news with his staff, parents, and community.

The diverse high school of 2,500 students had been experiencing an increase in fights over the years and some parents in the suburban community were calling on the school to focus more on school security. Utilizing national data on school safety, Principal Hubert drafted a message to parents announcing Officer Bensen's hire, highlighting his years of service on the police force, and restating the school's commitment to creating a safe school environment.

The letter was mailed home, placed on the school's website, and subsequently picked up by a local community newspaper that featured a profile of Officer Bensen. Asked to describe how he saw his new role as SRO, Officer Bensen was quoted in the article as saying that his new position as SRO at Duluth High School would be an extension of his role in the community. He remarked that as SRO he would employ many of the tactics and strategies that made him a successful career police officer.

Days later, Principal Hubert received a number of phone calls and emails from African American parents and community members expressing their concern over having a white police officer being hired as SRO. Some shared their fears of the "profiling" of black and brown students. Others who had lived in the community for many years recounted their unpleasant experiences with local police and wondered if the school administration was capable of monitoring the negative impact the decision might have on students of color.

Confused by the public outcry by some members of the community at his announcement, Principal Hubert sought the advice of Rev. Harold Gillespie, community advocate and pastor of a nearby African American church that many of his students attended. What had he missed? Why would the idea of increasing safety and creating a more secure school environment make people so upset?

Ultimately, Rev. Gillespie explained, African American parents were in support of keeping schools safe. However, they were viewing the decision through the lens of their own negative personal experiences with police, exacerbated by recent national news stories of police brutality against people of color. While these parents welcomed the "idea" of a school resource officer they were unable to connect a feeling of safety to a police presence. Rev. Gillespie inquired if Principal Hubert had mentioned in the correspondence how the school would build trust between students and SRO Bensen. Had he detailed in his letter what type of training the officer would receive to assist with socializing him into the school culture? Did he survey students, both Black and White, to learn how they felt about the new position and understand their concerns?

As Principal Hubert sought to answer these critical questions, he realized that he had not fully taken the time to understand his audiences. He had neglected to do the important work of collecting data and asking the right questions to help him interpret the perceptions, cultural connections, and current and historical perspectives necessary to communicate effectively with all his school's stakeholders.

STARTING WITH YOUR AUDIENCE

When it comes to school communication, most of the conversations and planning tend to focus on the tactics of a campaign—what it is that your school will be doing to communicate about the issue. That includes items like changing up the digital sign at the front of campus, developing a printed flier to send home with students, or perhaps an automated text that goes to family members.

While those decisions are important, your audience should be what drives what and how you communicate on a given topic. For example, imagine a principal is concerned about a rash of break-ins and vandalism during breaks. They are used to sending out an email to families, so they decide to use that method. In addition to the loss of property, administrators are also concerned about the amount of work it takes for staff to clean up after these incidents and these are the messages in the email.

This approach would be highly relevant for the families who live close enough to the campus to notice when there is something happening on campus and also happen to have a lot of empathy for the school staff. They would be highly likely to give that principal the behavior outcome they are looking for, calling the authorities when they see or hear something that's not quite right.

However, if that principal had considered the ideal audience for this issue, they may have proceeded differently. For example, the people who live within a certain radius of the campus are those that would be most likely to notice an incident. Perhaps only 20 percent of them actually have a child attending that school, with the rest being elderly homeowners. In the scenario above, 80 percent of the people that could be the most helpful would not have received the message.

Speaking of the message, while many people rightly care a great deal about school staff, the most effective way to universally reach folks is by appealing to their self-interest. What do the people who live around the school have in common? They are taxpayers, and their taxes are what pay for many of the resources on the campus. Messaging around protecting the community's investment so that their tax dollars aren't wasted on repairs is likely going to be more effective than the staff time approach.

In either case, one of the most important things the message can do is include a clear and easy call to action. In this case, it is requesting that they notify a specific agency and include the ways that they can contact that agency. The easier it is for someone to take that action step, the more likely they are to do it.

Lastly, choosing the right method to get the message to the audience is just as important as the development of the message. For the elderly campus neighbors, that principal may need to invest up front with home visits. A personal interaction with these neighbors will build credibility as well as allow the principal to obtain additional information, like their preferences for communication and addresses or email addresses for future messaging.

If that sounds like a lot of work, it is. However, the investment will return benefits over and over again—with a stronger relationship to the campus, this new audience are potential volunteers, donors, and voters. And if they are able to prevent or interrupt future break-ins and vandalism, how much time will that save everyone involved?

While it is tempting to slap together a quick message and send it out in a typical channel like email or text, school-site staff that are responsible for communication are usually responsible for much more than that and have limited time and resources. General messages don't work as well as those that are targeted for specific audiences. It makes sense to use a targeted approach and direct that time to the most effective message and channel possible.

So, what are some sample audiences that campus leaders should keep in mind? It depends on the issue, but below are some ideas to get you started.

- Students and subsections of students (grade, special program, neighborhood)
- Families and subsections of families (grade, neighborhood)
- Teaching staff and subsections of teaching staff (grade level, years in the school, or working with a special program)

- Support staff and subsections of support staff (function, neighborhood)
- District leaders
- District staff
- Board members
- Community leaders
- Voters
- Unconnected community members
- Campus neighbors
- Local business leaders
- Religious leaders
- Social service networks
- School alumni
- School or district retirees

IDENTIFY YOUR AUDIENCES

So how do you decide your key audiences for your campaign? It begins with research. Based on what you learn about your issue, try to identify those audiences that have the greatest potential impact. They usually fall into two categories—those who will be the most affected by the issue and those who have the most influence with those who will be affected.

For example, in the vandalism and break-in scenario, the neighbors who border the campus have the greatest potential impact on the issue. They are the most likely to notice an incident and be able to report it quickly.

Sometimes the answer is not so obvious. For a campaign to increase enrollment to a middle school, fourth and fifth grade students were brought into an informal focus group to talk about how they were making a decision about which middle school to attend. While the staff leading the discussion expected to hear about parental influence or specialized programs that were being offered, one of the surprising findings in the sessions was that peers were commonly listed at the top of the decision list—that is to say that these students were most concerned about where their friends were going to school.

How did that change the campaign? There was still outreach to students and families about the programs and strengths of the campus, but in addition the middle school developed a target marketing approach for each feeder elementary school. They sent their students back to the elementary schools they attended to host rallies about middle school and the programs that they were participating in that made school fun. They also handed out middle school "swag," such as pencils, t-shirts, and so on, to get the younger elementary students excited about moving on to their school.

These assemblies were attended by students of all ages at the elementary level, and got students talking about the strengths of the middle school. They saw neighborhood kids, perhaps the older siblings of their friends, as credible sources of information about middle school and the campaign turned the tide of neighborhood students choosing their campus.

So in the enrollment campaign, the audiences were the elementary students and staff from kindergarten through fifth grade and fourth and fifth grade families. In addition, the middle school provided marketing material about their campus for display in the lobby of each elementary campus and spoke at elementary staff meetings to highlight their campus strengths.

GATHERING INFORMATION

Once you've identified your audiences, it is important to try to gather as much information as possible about them to help decisions about messaging and channels. This doesn't have to be an extensive formal research project; any effort to increase understanding of the audiences in a campaign will improve communication efforts.

These efforts can include something as simple as asking a couple questions of family members as they drop off or pick up students in the morning. Or perhaps giving the office staff a question to ask each person who calls or emails the campus for a week (also noting their connection to the campus).

Any gathering of people can become an impromptu focus group, from students sitting together at lunch to staff members hanging out at happy hour. Having a couple of focused questions and leaving plenty of room for audience-driven discussions can provide a great deal of insight about what your audiences care about and how they are communicating.

If conducting a survey, closed-ended questions are the easiest to quickly analyze. For example, providing a list of ways that they prefer to receive information about the school and allowing them to select from that list. Open-ended questions are more time-consuming to analyze but often provide leaders with information they didn't already have.

There is a variety of information that might be helpful to collect from audience members and there are several factors that impact the decision about what to collect. The first is the demographic information that influences audience attitudes about the issue. For example, does the age, gender, socioeconomic status, sexual orientation, culture, race, or other group membership detail affect the way this audience feels about the new social studies curriculum?

The second factor is how intrusive the questioning might be perceived. The level of trust the audience has with the school staff as a direct influence on the level of intimacy of questions that might be appropriate in a given situation. Not sure? Ask a sample of the audience what they think about your question. If in doubt, leave it out. It is more important to collect some information than attempt to get everything you think you need and risk alienating your audience before your campaign has even started.

The third factor is the length of the survey or other research activity. Think of your research as a scale. On the one side, you have the things you want to learn. On the other side, you have the attention span of your audience. The more questions you add, the less likely your audience is to complete your survey.

Beyond demographics, consider asking about other areas that impact how an audience might perceive your campaign—their current attitude about your issue, the way that they receive information in general, and who they trust to speak about your issue.

While this sounds like additional work on a plate that may already be full, keep in mind that most schools are routinely reaching out to their key audiences again and again. The research that is conducted can be helpful in subsequent communication efforts and doesn't need to be replicated for each campaign.

In fact, it may be helpful to develop a generic survey of demographics, psychographics, and communication preferences that is administered each year to help stay current and identify potential trends. This takes some up-front work, but saves time in the long run when leaders are able to identify channels that are no longer preferred, or attitudes that are changing in a negative direction.

ASK & ANSWER

- Who are my stakeholders?
- Do all of them view the issue/concern the same way I see it?
- Who would be a good thought partner to discuss this with?
- Is there any current trend, public perception, or item in the news that relates to this topic?

Supplemental training materials available for this chapter at www.schoolprpro.com/the-communicating-principal.

FIVE

Planning Your Work

The Scranton Education Center (SEC) is an alternative education program that provides a unique educational experience for students who require a broader range of academic, behavioral, and social-emotional interventions. Students receive the benefit of non-traditional teaching, therapeutic support, and online courses. The program's goal is to help students secure the required credits to graduate high school and become independent citizens.

Principal Jonathan Cooper recognized that even though his teachers and social services staff were committed to their students, the future for many attending SEC remained uncertain. Plus, in recent years, community perceptions and support for the school had started to wane.

In early 2017, Principal Cooper's program received a state grant that allowed him to purchase new printing equipment for his print shop class. He soon realized that hands-on learning was having a positive impact on students who were usually tardy or absent. The idea for a student entrepreneurship program was slowly taking shape and nearly one year later the Scranton Artisan Workshop was born.

The workshop produced printed items such as t-shirts, mugs, greeting cards, posters, stationery, and magnets. The student-run print shop employed approximately fourteen students who received class credit for attending each day on time. Principal Cooper became excited at the prospect of the workshop expanding its reach within the community.

He began with the creation of a business plan. The document required him to gather research on everything from workforce development models to the cost of materials.

This collection of data greatly assisted his staff in not only understanding the project's business objectives but also the program's purpose and vision. Next, he began meeting with teaching staff to discuss logistics, classroom scheduling, and day-to-day operations. He assembled key administrative staff to lead teams through an analysis of how the entrepreneurship program could provide work-force skills while ensuring students continued to meet their educational objectives.

Finally, Principal Cooper enlisted the help of student artists to create a logo and brochure about the program. Armed with a small budget, he began a communications blitz that included writing an article in the district's newsletter, placing an ad on the website, and inviting a reporter from the local community newspaper to visit the school. Sensing momentum, Principal Cooper hosted a Community Open House with tours of the workshop led by students, after which guests were invited to play games and win printed items featuring the program's logo.

As a result of this year-long effort, students were invited by a successful business owner in the community to attend the local chamber of commerce meeting. School administrators agreed to use the workshop for some of their office print jobs, and interest in the program is spreading. With solid research and planning school leaders can create campaigns that promote innovative initiatives, energize staff, and market student success.

Most television shows and movies that include a public relations professional leave viewers with the impression that PR people come up with brilliant campaigns at a moment's notice and based exclusively on their intuition. The real genius behind most PR campaigns is in the planning. Is it built on a foundation of accurate information, does it consider the audiences, and does it include messaging and tactics specific to those audiences?

Fortunately, there is an established four-step process that can serve as guidance in the development of an effective plan. While there are multiple variations on the names for the process, the steps are basically the same. The two most common are RPIE and RACE. R-P-I-E lists the steps as: research, planning, implementation, and evaluation. The R-A-C-E approach also starts with research and ends with evaluation, but identifies analysis and communication as the second and third steps. Either approach, as outlined in table 5.1, is a helpful tool in creating a thoughtful approach to public relations work.

RESEARCH

It's no coincidence that research is the first step in almost any PR process. Understanding as much as possible about an issue, the impacted audiences, and their communication preferences is a foundational step. It is like the concrete slab underneath a house—if it's not solid, it's impossible to build a sturdy structure.

For example, developing a plan to improve enrollment at a middle school might include looking at the enrollment trends in the regional area

Table 5.1.

RACE	RPIE	Step Descriptions
	Research	• Define challenge, concern, or opportunity—one-time situation or ongoing? • Describe desired situation • Use primary, secondary, qualitative, quantitative, formal, and/or informal research • Supportive and challenging forces • Who is involved and/or affected and how? • Who is influential?
Analysis	Planning	• Audiences the program should reach and affect—don't forget internal audiences • Define specifically—demographics, psychographics, behavior toward messages/issues • What should be achieved with each public to accomplish the program goal • Four parts: audience, behavior/action, measurement, and timeframe • Changes needed to achieve the outcomes in the objectives • Message content that must be communicated to each audience to achieve the outcomes stated in the objectives • Media/channels that best reach the target publics
Communication	Implementation	• Specific tools steps needed for each strategy—website, event, brochure, Facebook, eNews story, Op-ed, etc. • Staff responsible for implementing each tactic • Sequence of events and schedule • Costs of each tactic—don't forget time, subscriptions, materials
	Evaluation	• How outcomes specified in the goals and objectives will be measured—e.g., vote, attendance, open rate, survey response, etc. • How results will be reported to management teams and used to make the program better

and surveying families and students about what they are looking for in a school and what social media platforms they utilize. Using that information as a starting point will ensure personalized, persuasive messaging, and effective tools and tactics.

PLANNING/ANALYSIS

The planning/analysis step brings together the information collected through the foundational research in the development of a comprehensive plan. The plan should address the primary audiences/stakeholders. This would include the groups of people most affected by the particular issue as well as potential influencers—groups or individuals that others may turn to as an authority on the topic.

Internal audiences, such as school secretaries, can serve as highly effective influencer groups on a variety of issues. They interact with classified support staff on the campus and at the district office, as well as site teachers, students, and families.

When thinking through both primary and secondary/influencer audiences, it is important to take note of specific demographics and psychographics. For example, demographics might include language spoken, socioeconomic status, internet access, and neighborhood—basically anything that answers the question of who they are.

Psychographics provide a window into what the group thinks and why. Understanding through the results of a survey that fifth grade students are heavily influenced by their peers on the topic of which middle school to attend is extremely helpful psychographic information.

The plan should also include campaign objectives for each audience. What should be achieved with each to accomplish the campaign goal and how will it be measured? Truly measurable objectives include four parts—the audience, the behavior change, how the behavior will be measured, and the timeframe in which the change will happen.

The campaign strategies and tactics round out the plan. This would include the key messages, the channels that best reach each target audience, and the specific tools needed for each strategy. The tactics section is a granular description of the action to be taken and might include a website, an event, a fact sheet, a Facebook advertisement, or another tool as identified as potentially effective for the audience.

COMMUNICATION/IMPLEMENTATION

Once the plan is fleshed out, the next step is the one most visible to the outside world. The communication/implementation step is what you typically see reflected in television and movie portrayals of PR. It is where the detailed plan is enacted—the events are held, the tweets are sent out, and the email is written and sent off.

While it is a distinct phase for the purposes of planning, there is still a great deal of planning, measuring, and tracking happening during this step. If the outputs are not showing the results we expect, we don't have to wait until the evaluation to change course.

Are your tweets not getting enough engagement? Take another look at the message—is it tailored for the audience? Is it tailored for Twitter? Pull in a few members of the intended audience and brainstorm some tweaks to the message or think about changing tactics altogether, shifting your time and energy.

EVALUATION

In many cases, the implementation is the end of the campaign story. For most school leaders, they are off and running to the next issue (or five) at their door. However, if we don't take the time to review our efforts, it is difficult to learn what worked and what didn't.

For example, did more people attend the event this year? How did they find out about the event? If none of the people that attend report that they heard about it through the expensive and time-consuming printed newsletter, maybe it's time to cut back on the number of issues each year or stop it altogether so that more time and resources are available for more effective communication tools.

PUTTING IT ALL TOGETHER: A PLAN

If the idea of developing a communication plan for your campus seems out of reach, take heart. There is no perfect format for a plan; it doesn't need to be a certain number of pages or in a special binder to be effective.

The most important aspect of a plan is in developing one that works for your circumstances. Too long, and no one will read or refer back to it, too short and it won't contain the details you need to stay on track. It can be helpful to think of your communication plan as a work plan built on research.

For example, your plan can be as simple as a short background on the issue that explains what you know (research) along with the actions you are going to take to reach each audience and how you will measure the effectiveness of each action. See below.

STEM LAB CAMPAIGN EXAMPLE

Background: The new STEM lab at ABC middle school was built as a result of survey results that indicated that the majority of elementary families and students in the area were most interested in STEM-related careers and preparation.

Audience One: Fifth Grade Parents

- Informational email and invitation February 15 evaluated by open rates and replies
- Parent information night on March 15 evaluated by attendance rate
- Email follow-up with flier attachment evaluated by open rates and replies

Audience Two: Local Real Estate Agents

- Informational email and invitation May 15 evaluated by open rates and replies
- Parent information night on June 15 evaluated by attendance rate
- Email follow-up with flier attachment evaluated by open rates and replies

Overall Evaluation

- Fall attendance rates
- Survey of new students indicating reasons for choice and how they heard about the program

As evidenced in this simple plan, it doesn't take a lot of time and effort to be more mindful about how time and resources are spent in public relations campaigns. All of these steps, from research to evaluation, play a role in the long-term success of a school's communication efforts. Understanding of the community, school-related issues, and communication preferences will continue to grow and the people conducting the campaigns will develop more and more sophistication and depth.

A sample communication plan template that can be downloaded and edited for immediate use is available at www.schoolprpro.com/the-communicating-principal.

While the planning process may not be an exciting component of an hour-long sitcom, in real life the most successful PR campaigns are the ones who spend a great deal of time conducting and looking at research, analyzing and planning out campaigns, and evaluating how well campaigns performed so they can be even more effective next time.

ASK & ANSWER

- What key messages need to be shared with your stakeholders for them to understand the educational impact of your campaign?
- Is the timeline you've set achievable?
- Have you identified internal/external individuals or groups who would partner with you to support the effort? Spread the word?

Supplemental training materials available for this chapter at www.schoolprpro.com/the-communicating-principal.

SIX

Messaging

The look on her secretary's face said it all. Something was very wrong. As the new director of the Early Childhood Program, Juanita Lopez was usually the first one in and the last one out. "We just received a call from a parent saying that the neighbor she asked to pick up her student was given the wrong child!"

Immediately, Ms. Lopez instructed her secretary to contact the local police department and quickly locate the student's teacher, Ms. Adams. The teacher explained that the parent was working late and asked a neighbor to pick up her daughter, Jasmine, from school. Unaware that there were two students in the dismissal area named Jasmine, the paraprofessional on duty mistakenly gave the neighbor the wrong child.

Minutes later, after realizing the error, the neighbor returned to the school with the student. She admitted to answering a text message at the time and not paying close attention to detect the mix-up. After speaking to the mother of the student about the error, Ms. Lopez planned to send a heartfelt letter of apology to the family the next day.

However, within one hour of the incident, a social media post exposing the story began circulating. With a flood of Facebook posts expressing shock, horror, and outrage at the school and its staff, she knew that she was about to write the most critical parent letter of her career.

Before composing the letter, Ms. Lopez decided to refer back to social media comments and ask herself some hard questions. Why were people really angry? What could have been done to prevent it? What system or process needed to be fixed, and how?

As she opened the letter with a retelling of the incident (to correct rumors), she was sure to accept full responsibility for what happened while resisting the impulse to make the letter all about the apology. Ms. Lopez clearly outlined for parents where the missteps occurred and described in a detailed, bulleted list what procedures should have been followed. While she was careful not to throw

*her staff "under the bus," she upheld her role as a leader by assuring parents that
there would be a review and training.*

*Most importantly, her tone communicated to parents that she was a caring
leader who did not take their trust lightly. She avoided clichés like "The safety of
our students is our highest priority" and used language that affirmed one of the
biggest fears for parents of small children.*

*Finally, rather than simply assure parents that the problem would be solved,
Ms. Lopez invited them to visit the school at any time to observe the new dismissal procedures in action. School leaders like Ms. Lopez remind us that the best
messages require humility, honesty, and the courage to see your organization
from the outside-in rather than from the inside out.*

School leaders are often called upon to communicate about challenging
circumstances. Whether it is the bad behavior of an employee, the unrea-
sonable demands of negotiating groups, or a high-profile crisis, the way
that you communicate can define the school for years to come. In addition, the way that a campus leadership team communicates on a regular
basis impacts the level of trust stakeholders have in the school as well as
the effectiveness of proactive, positive messaging.

CRISIS MESSAGING

As part of the larger society, a school is bound to face some of the same
challenges that affect people everywhere. Effectively communicating
when things go wrong is incredibly important. Situations are tense, and
everyone is under a microscope. When the thing that goes wrong is your
own employee behavior, it makes communicating even tougher.

Whether it is something small like petty theft or something much
larger like an accusation about hurting a child, it is important to consider
all the stakeholders involved in the issue. Employees will be watching to
see if the treatment of the accused employee is fair and taking into consideration the rights of the employee.

Families and the community will be watching to see if you are doing
enough to protect children. Obviously, one of the most important things
that should happen immediately in the case of an accusation of a hurt
child is removing the employee from any scenario where they might
come into contact with children. The wording that is used during this
time period is important as well. An accusation, no matter how abhor-
rent, is only an accusation and needs to be described as such until more is
known.

The process of looking into the accusation is often referred to as an
investigation. This is a problematic term unless it is used by a law enforcement agency. Reviewing the accusation and the facts related to it is
more neutral terminology and doesn't imply schools have investigative

authority. Fully cooperating with law enforcement and turning the accusation and related facts over to the local investigative agency is another important element to communicate to stakeholders.

You should be prepared to answer some basic questions when communicating about an employee issue:

- What happened—when you found out about it, what you did
- What does the law say about the potential infraction as well as employee privacy?
- How are you taking care of students?
- How are you taking care of staff?

In developing proactive messaging around the issue, it is important to also bring other perspectives into the discussion. Think through the variety of stakeholders that might be impacted or concerned about this issue and bring in trusted representatives of those groups to help with message development. This ensures leaders are less likely to unintentionally leave out important information.

In crisis message-development meetings, the agenda should include developing a list of questions people might have and developing a list of everyone who might need to answer questions. As part of the discussion, it may be helpful to formally assign someone to play the devil's advocate to ask tough questions.

When the crisis messaging is ready, reach out to the people who will likely be asked questions on the topic and share the points that the group developed. It is almost always a good idea to ensure that internal audiences are prepared with messaging before it is shared with external stakeholders like families, media, and the community.

When the questions do come, there are a few specific tips to keep in mind. One of the most important is not falling into the trap of answering a hypothetical scenario question. For example, a member of the media may ask, "What will happen if the employee is found guilty?"

Rather than answer that type of question, it is a better idea to stay in the present moment and decline to guess at a hypothetical set of conditions. Using a bridging statement like, "Right now, we are focused on the learning conditions of our students and ensuring their needs are met" can change the discussion to matters that are actually currently in the control of the school leader.

There are times when it is strategic for a school leader to send a message that the school is taking the issues seriously while still avoiding any discussion that infringes on the privacy of the accused employee. There are a couple of ways to talk about policies or procedures in general that provide loose guidance. For example, a school leader could say, "I can't speak to this specific case, however in general . . ." or they could say, "In a case where a person was suspected of — —, our policy is to — —."

There are also times when it isn't possible to give the community or media the information they are asking about. In that case, it is important not just to say "no comment" or decline to answer the question. Explaining the exact nature of the law that leaders are following is important to maintain trust with skeptical audiences. An example might be, "We cannot share this information because the law [name it if appropriate] requires us to protect the privacy of our staff/students."

REAL APOLOGIES

One of the most important messages a school leader will write is an apology. As an organization run by humans, it is inevitable that mistakes will be made. What a leader does immediately following a mistake can make or break their reputation for a very long time.

When something happens, there is always some tension between how quickly to get information out and how accurate that information should be. For example, sometimes after an incident like a confrontation on campus, it may take a couple of days of interviewing to discover exactly what happened between a staff member and a student. It is not likely that a school community will be satisfied to wait that long before they hear from their school leader on the topic.

One of the ways to address the time/accuracy conundrum is by using language that only specifically refers to what you know. For example, "This is what we know so far about what happened" or "We received a complaint about" or "We were notified about" without confirming facts that you are not yet sure about. Of course, the rest of the messaging should include how students are being taken care of, what the next steps are, and when people can expect additional information.

The elements of a real apology include: concern about the situation or accusation, addressing what the campus is doing for student health and safety, an apology listing specifically what the school did or precisely what the student or staff member experienced, a solution that includes the steps that will be taken to ensure it doesn't happen again, and resources for those who are affected or want to learn more.

Concern about the situation or accusation: another element that is sometimes lacking in apology messages is emotion. Here we face yet another tension, that between caring about what happened and the legal implications of accepting responsibility. This is a healthy tension, and both sides should be represented at the messaging table to ensure the right balance is struck.

There is often plenty of middle ground in which a school leader can be deeply troubled, saddened, or shocked about an incident without implying legal responsibility. It is a critical element of an apology, and if it is missing, the messaging can come off as inauthentic, robotic, bureaucratic, or worse.

Address what the campus is doing for student health and safety: the most important question that families will have during an incident is, are their children safe? It is extremely important that immediate steps are taken to remove children from any potential harm and meet their health and safety needs. Those steps need to be communicated in the apology message, along with:

1. Apology listing specifically what the school did or specifically what the student or staff member experienced: don't be afraid to be honest in describing what happened, focusing on the pain or harm that was experienced, regardless of whether or not your school or district is responsible. If people don't see an honest accounting of the incident, they are less likely to believe the apology.

2. A solution that includes the steps that will be taken to ensure it doesn't happen again: outline the steps you are taking and changes you are making in policy, protocols, training, communication, or staffing that will prevent this negative thing from happening again. If you are not yet sure of the specific changes, let people know what you are reviewing and when they can expect an update from you.

3. Resources for those who are affected or want to learn more: one nice way to end a crisis message by demonstrating that your main concern is people is to share with them the resources that are available. The resources can be something your school or district provides, a link to additional information, or contact information for community agencies that help in that area. For more guidance on crisis communication strategies and messaging, see chapters 7 and 8.

PROACTIVE MESSAGING

The messaging a campus team sends out on a regular basis has a great deal of influence over how they will fare when a crisis comes along. It is imperative that messaging is internal first, timely, and responsive to audience differences.

Even when a campus leader has a strong, positive vision and is communicating effectively with families, they can sometimes get in trouble by leap-frogging over internal staff with important information. A good rule of thumb is to communicate inside-out (after district leaders are informed). Think of a pond when a pebble is thrown into it, and imagine the circles that ripple outward. A school's communication plan should be the same—communicating first with those closest to campus like teaching and support staff then students and families, and lastly, general community or media. No one should hear new information about their campus through a third party.

A side benefit of this inside-out approach to messaging is that it builds a team of internal information sources who can help with questions and share the information in their circles of influence, which can be much more powerful than a generic email or flier.

Messaging must also be timely. That means being proactive about responding to a crisis, but it is also just as essential to respect the time of your staff and families by providing information in a time period that is realistically actionable. For example, if you are inviting people to events with less than two weeks' notice, it can be inconsiderate to those who have to try to rearrange their plans in order to participate in the event.

When a campus is considering changes, that timeliness becomes even more important. If it is a particularly busy time of the year and new software needs to be implemented (not recommended), it is essential that people are given as much notice as possible about the change that is coming. Ideally, there is an opportunity to allow them to weigh in on the change before it is decided.

Messaging should be specific to your audiences and take their differences into consideration. When developing a message for staff, it may be important to include educational jargon or district-specific language about initiatives. However, when putting together a message for families with limited English language skills, it is important to review messaging and ensure that it is clear and free of jargon that might make it confusing to non-educators.

One of the main reasons that there is so much time spent upfront identifying and researching audiences is so that the messaging that is developed is responsive to cultural, language, educational, and other differences within specific audiences. Think through word choices to ensure that your messaging is inclusive and detailed.

Also, think about the relevance to the audience. While all the stakeholders in a school community care about students and learning, each audience might have a different concern or aspiration related to your issue. For example, when discussing an early out day for professional development, staff are likely wondering how much of that time they will be given for personal preparation, while many families might be wondering if there is after-school care available.

In the end, it is about being intentional about the words that are selected for your messaging. They should have a tone that reflects your school values, rather than be a neutral reciting of information. For example, if your campus prides itself on unity and togetherness, the language in your message should reflect that value and use phrasing like "our school," "our campus," "our families," "our community," and "our district" rather than using the word "the" before each of these.

The way to tailor messaging is as unique as school campuses are, but the most important element is to be thoughtful about your audience and mindful as you are crafting messages for them. There are also several ways to reduce the amount of work this will take.

REDUCE, REUSE, RECYCLE

As a campus leader, you likely need to be very organized. That upcoming Open House event is planned down to the last detail—from the welcome speech and PTA recruitment table to the fifth grade snack booth. You wouldn't dream of running your school any other way, and yet you may not have a plan when it comes to one of the most important campus functions, communicating with families and other stakeholder groups.

It doesn't have to be lengthy, formal, or overly complicated, but giving some thought to creating a simple, system-wide plan for communicating will increase the effectiveness of your communication efforts and save you a lot of time throughout the year.

While it is tempting to try to create communication across various methods, it can take a lot of time and attention. You'll need to be able to narrow your list to those that are most likely to reach your audiences. If you don't know what that list should be, a simple survey of families could be an excellent place to start. Don't have time for a survey? Include it as part of the check-in sheet for your next event. Add a column for each communication tool and have family members mark the methods they prefer to receive communication from you.

It can be enormously helpful to ask families to delineate how they prefer to be notified for urgent/crisis matters versus school news and information. In addition, confirm the contact information that a school has in the system for family members.

Once you have your basic plan pulled together, there are a few easy tips that can help you implement the plan throughout the year and save time in the process. Think of it as a communication conservation process: reduce, reuse, and recycle.

First, reduce the amount you are writing. Attention spans are shrinking, and your messages are competing with more content than ever before. Consider using bullets and links to additional information for larger stories. Graphics or photos with captions can sometimes cover a topic more effectively than an article and also add overall visual interest. Add subheadlines throughout your document to ensure that families can quickly scan the material and hone in on the items that most affect them.

Secondly, reuse your content. If you've created an email for families, you should use the same content for your website, Facebook, or Twitter account. If you're using a tool that is more visual in nature, like social media, use a photo or graphic with a short description linking to the larger article. To see a sample content calendar demonstrating this concept, check out the book's supplemental materials at www.schoolprpro.com/the-communicating-principal.

Create a checklist of the communication tools you'll be using for the year to help you remember to distribute the content in a variety of ways. The checklist is also something you can plan to bring to meetings with staff and families, using it to brainstorm how you will get information out on a topic under discussion.

Lastly, recycle your content. Like most schools, you likely have events that every year at about the same time. Rather than recreate the content each year, recycle the content you used the year before, and change the dates. People will not notice that it's the same story, but if you feel you must update it, changing the graphics will likely be enough to make it feel fresh again.

To make it even easier to recycle content for next year, create a spreadsheet and copy and paste your content from each event. Use different tabs for each month to make it easier to find the following year. If you're technologically savvy, consider using the website If This Then That (IFTTT) and set up an autosave from your communication tools to a Google spreadsheet.

IN SUMMARY

Ensuring that your messaging is consistent, strategic, and authentic will go a long way in helping you set and communicate a vision for where the campus or district is going. Schools are a mirror of the communities around them and will face many of the same challenges. Strong communication means having the systems and messaging in place to allow you to lead on important issues.

Like most of the things discussed in this book, it will take more time upfront, but the good news is that this is another area of increasing benefits over time. Trust is built through consistent, effective communication.

ASK & ANSWER

- Have you reviewed your plan for disseminating time-sensitive information?
- Are you a leader who relies on or rejects soft skills when communicating with internal/external audiences?
- Do you develop messages based on hard facts or information from people you deem believable?

Supplemental training materials available for this chapter at www.schoolprpro.com/the-communicating-principal.

Part III

Implementation

SEVEN

Communication Channels

After years of long lines, long waits, and reams of color-coded forms, registration for all new and returning students would now be completed online. Townsend High School (THS) Principal Mark Kinzie was excited about the change. For years, he dreaded those three weeks at the end of summer when his building would be filled with parents and their students waiting in lines to register and pay fees.

In an effort to streamline the process, parents and guardians could now log on to the school district's website to upload documents, sign forms, and pay fees. It would be fast, simple, and not require that his secretary be buried under a sea of papers, folders, and forms.

In the months leading up to registration, Mr. Kinzie asked his administrative assistant, Carrie, to send out a weekly reminder to parents that online registration would be starting soon. A week into the new online registration process, Mr. Kinzie asks his assistant Carrie to generate a report showing how many THS families had already registered. "Not as many as you'd think," she said dubiously.

Mr. Kinzie was perplexed. He was certain that the ease of the new online registration system was just what his parents had been waiting for. But nearly two weeks had passed and there were still a considerable lack of responses. Mr. Kinzie decided to ask Carrie to log into the online portal. Interestingly, it appeared that while many families had started the process, the incomplete registration rate was incredibly high.

He wanted to know why. After calls to at least a dozen households, Mr. Kinzie was surprised to learn that his families found the new online system cumbersome and confusing. For others who lacked technical savvy, having to scan documents and create portable file documents (.PDF) proved prohibitive. Some even mentioned the lack of Wi-Fi at home as being a reason not to register online.

After some additional analysis, he realized that his assumptions about how parents would respond to the new technology were flawed. They didn't take into account the end users' home computer systems, broadband connections, or bandwidth to follow a list of detailed written instructions.

His immediate next step was to reach out to his director of IT to create a plan for parents to access the Help Desk for assistance. They arranged for fifteen-minute time slots for parents to call in to receive personalized assistance from a member of the Technology Team. While this new step in the process added additional time to complete registration, parents were less anxious at the prospect of having a live person to help them register their student.

One of the most important decisions a leader will make is the communication channels that they choose to get a message out. Understanding the intended audience is the first step. Using the communication channels an audience is already using is an effective way to ensure that your message will get to them.

There are also a number of channels that are unique to a school system. Most leaders have access to automated calling and texting, which can be very effective tools because they go directly to the mobile phones that most people have with them.

School website content can be a little trickier. It is more passive and usually requires a complementary communication tool to proactively reach out to let audiences know that the information has been posted. In this chapter, we'll discuss a variety of communication channels along with the potential strengths and weaknesses of using each.

FACE-TO-FACE

Description: Face-to-face communication is repeatedly demonstrated to be the most powerful type of communication there is. When it comes to choosing a new service or product, hearing a positive review from someone you know is marketing gold. The same holds true for schools. Survey after survey reveals that families depend on the opinions of the people in their lives—playdate parents, soccer coaches, and people who attend the same church—are the most trusted "spokespeople" or "influencers" in their lives.

While it is the most powerful way to communicate with people, it is also the most time-consuming, particularly if it takes place one on one. While it should be a part of every communication strategy, it needs to be supplemented with a variety of other methods in order to meet the informational needs of today's world.

The options for face-to-face communication vary based on size, goal, formality, and frequency of occurrence. For example, a weekly or monthly informal gathering with the principal is a great way to listen to daily concerns or suggestions.

Formal advisory groups, on the other hand, require more planning and preparation. While they might meet monthly throughout the year, they can also be pulled together for a limited period of time to work on a time-sensitive project like an event or collaborate on guidance for a given topic that can be provided to a leadership team as they are making a decision. In order for that guidance to be broadly useful, leaders must ensure that advisory groups are representative of larger community populations.

School-based forums and special community meetings are one-time or limited series forums to provide and obtain information on a specific topic. They also require the development of a thoughtful agenda that provides plenty of time for questions and answers to take full advantage of the in-person format. If the topic is potentially heated and a large number of people are expected, it may also be a good idea to consider breaking the larger forum into small groups facilitated by trained staff members or volunteers to provide ample opportunities to provide critical feedback and discuss concerns.

In all of these face-to-face events, it is important to consider supports and materials that ensure an equal opportunity to participate. For example, if there are families in the community who speak a language other than English, consider providing translated materials and live interpretation. If the cost of those items is not in the budget, consider asking for volunteers in the community who can donate interpretation and translation services.

If it is an evening meeting, consider making it easier for families to attend by offering play-care activities for younger children and a meal or refreshments. For some families, there may not be an adult available for childcare and they have to come straight from work to arrive at an event. Removing barriers that can get in the way of participation can help ensure a wider variety of voices and input. When possible, include a variety of times to participate so that families and community members with different schedules can find a time that works for them.

Pros: By all measures, face-to-face communication is the most powerful channel that can be used. When listening to a message in person from a trusted leader or peer, people are far more likely to understand and support a new idea or initiative.

In addition, feedback from audience participants is immediate. Even if that feedback is nonverbal, a school leader will get an idea very quickly about how an idea or response on an issue is likely to be received. They also have an immediate opportunity to dive more deeply into the issue to find out where a disconnect might be.

Is it the language being used to frame the issue? Is it the perceived lack of involvement in the decision-making process? Is it a concern that students or families will be treated inequitably as a result? Working through these items face-to-face allows a leader to carefully consider decisions, actions, and language through the lens of audience perception.

Cons: As powerful as face-to-face communication can be, it is also the most time-consuming. Unless it is a very large crowd (which takes away from some of the benefits of immediacy), there is a much different ratio of time spent to people reached than some of the digital options a school might have at their disposal.

In addition to being time-consuming, it might not always be possible. The COVID-19 outbreak in 2020 demonstrated that there may be societal issues that become barriers to this type of communication experience.

Most importantly, face-to-face communication requires a great deal of thought to ensure that it is equitable. For example, if a Principal Tea is held each Tuesday from 9:00 a.m. to 10:00 a.m., it is likely not possible that most working families can attend. It doesn't mean it shouldn't happen, but a leader could rotate to evenings every other occurrence to ensure equal opportunity to have a face-to-face conversation with the principal.

Lastly, remember that in-person meetings can be very difficult for people who identify as introverts. Not everyone feels comfortable speaking up in groups of people, even when they are smaller groups. Be sure to offer the opportunity for follow-up from others in the group with an email address or even a drop-box in the office. This ensures that there are more perspectives being taken into consideration—not just the loudest voices in the room.

PRINT

Description: Printed materials have been the traditional method of communication in schools for decades. The copy rooms of nearly every school in the country are filled with a rainbow of color choices to get the word out about fundraisers, back-to-school nights, or talent shows. However, as more and more staff and families become comfortable with digital communication, it has lost some favor.

For example, calendars have been the centerpiece of school communication for years. Figure out the annual schedule, and add all the dates to the calendar, as well as contact information for a variety of resources available through the school community.

Printed newsletters have also been a popular way to get the word out about campus events and celebrations. The content is collected, laid out, printed, and then sent home in student's backpacks. It is a good way to combine a variety of messages and information that affect many if not all members of the school community. It does require some time to collect the content from busy teachers, as well as some skill in laying out the text and photos. With the amount of effort required, print newsletters are usually provided on a monthly basis.

Flyers are simpler versions of newsletters and typically focus on just one topic. They can be used on a number of different topics, but a leader needs to be careful that audience members don't get inundated with flyers to the point that their value as a communication tool is lessened or lost. If families receive new flyers each day of the week, it can be tough to keep them straight. In that case, it may be better to combine the content and place it in a newsletter for easier access.

Pros: One of the strongest arguments in favor of using printed communication tools is that it provides more equity in terms of access to information if not all members of a school community have practical access to digital communication. Practical access means that not only do they technically have an email account but also that they have the technical experience, tools, internet access, and time it takes to go into an email account and access information.

Cons: Unfortunately, there are a lot of challenges associated with printed materials. It starts with the delivery of the materials to the home. Children's backpacks are notoriously unreliable methods of transport. If the materials do make it home, a family member may glance at it and then forget where they read a piece of information and are unable to look it up later as they would be able to do with digital communication.

In addition, once it is printed, materials begin to age. If something changes or was incorrect at the time of printing, it is impossible to update the printed versions that are sitting on dining room tables. Lastly, it is much more difficult to track the effectiveness of this type of tool. When something is communicated digitally, there is usually some type of data that can be collected to see if the email was opened or a link was clicked. It takes a secondary effort to discover if families received and read a newsletter.

DIGITAL

Description: There are a wide variety of digital tools available to school leaders, from email to website to digital signage. There are new avenues opening up in digital options every day. Many districts are taking advantage of online flyer distribution, automated texting, and online portals and applications. For the purposes of this book, social media, while technically digital in form, will be discussed as a separate item.

E-newsletters have become a very popular tool as a variety of companies have started making it relatively easy for non-designers to put together a quality electronic newsletter. In addition, some automated messaging systems have started offering their own solutions or partnering with third-party companies to offer easy templates that integrate with existing school systems.

In addition, many e-newsletter options offer the ability to include links back to the school website or other online resources, as well as track how people are interacting with the content. How many are opening? How many are clicking on each link? Who did recipients forward the e-newsletters to? There is a lot to be learned about reader behavior and content preferences by combing through the data.

Although it is nearly fifty years old as of the writing of this book, email remains a strong digital communication option. In fact, in response to the shrinking attention span and time of families, many schools and districts are shrinking their e-newsletter effort and turning instead to a weekly brief overview email. For example, a district in the bay area of California sends out a weekly "Five Things You Need to Know" from the superintendent and it includes the top five stories with a paragraph intro and photo and link to a longer website story.

There are a number of advantages to this tool, including the fact that recipients can easily find past emails by date and content through a search of their email. In addition, this active communication tool reaches out to people and informs them of the information available on a more passive tool, the website.

Even though most schools don't have a budget for a programmer or designer, well-designed and up-to-date school websites have become the expectation around the country. A school's website may be the first connection a potential family makes, so it is important that the site is welcoming, fresh with new and relevant information, and easy to navigate. Many first and second generations of websites were designed inside-out—the educators tasked with putting up a school website on top of the everyday work of running a school simply took the internal organization and posted it to the outside.

If you've discovered through the use of Google Analytics on your site or a survey of your families and staff that your website is not meeting their needs, it may be time to invest in some qualitative research—bringing stakeholder groups in and ask them questions about the site, then give them a few tasks to complete and have them talk you through where they would start and steps they would take on your site.

Also, talk to your frontline staff. A website can be an amazing resource for those who are typically answering the public's questions. If the top ten things they engage with the public about are listed on the website, it can significantly help with their workload, and then they can spend that time helping with website maintenance. With the school website tools available today, most people who are comfortable working with Google Docs or Microsoft Word documents will quickly catch on.

On the technologically advanced end of the spectrum at this time, schools and districts can add mobile applications that families and staff can download to their phones to receive information. These applications allow school leaders to slim down to the most important content organized in a way that makes sense to people outside the school system.

It can also provide a convenient way for families and staff to complete online tasks related to campus like filling out forms and completing surveys. Like other active digital tools, applications can serve as a great compliment to a website, getting the attention of application users and directing them to relevant information that might not be noticed otherwise.

While slower to market because of the recipient costs that used to be associated, auto texts have now become the most popular tools in a number of school systems. The key is to keep them brief, consistent, and relevant. Like it or not, nearly everyone has a mobile phone that is carried with them most of the day. The auto text tool is in some ways stronger than other platform-based digital tools because the recipient doesn't have to choose to download an application or subscribe to an email or e-newsletter.

Text notifications are immediate and light up phones in almost the same moment they are sent, making them a critical emergency notification tool. It is for that reason that leaders need to be careful about the overuse of this tool and avoid annoying people enough that they opt out of the texting subscription list. It is also important to research all relevant auto texting laws and guidelines that are relevant to your school at the district, state, and federal levels. Your state school public relations association would likely be a great source for this information.

Pros: There are a number of digital media strengths, starting with the timing. With most digital tools, a message can be crafted and sent within minutes to a large population. That decreases the probability that the information contained within the tool will be inaccurate. However, as we learned during the pandemic, things can change quickly. Luckily, digital media is more forgiving than print or face-to-face communication. In most cases, the content can be adjusted without most people noticing, or a revised email can be sent out as an update.

One of the biggest reasons to spend more effort on digital communication is that it is likely that is where your audiences are and it is easier to reach people where they are already receiving information than train them to look somewhere new. In addition, the analytics that are built into most digital tools are amazing sources of information for communication improvement.

Cons: It is important to point out that there are two different digital tool types—active and passive. Active tools push into people's lives and they receive an email, a text, or notification. A passive tool like a website (unless it allows a subscription for website changes) does not. Many leaders mistakenly believe that when they post information on their website that they have communicated with their stakeholder groups. As much as we would like them to, most folks are not regularly checking school websites for the latest information. That is where more active tools are a great compliment to a website.

It is also important to know your audience. If they are not using the tools you want to use, if they don't speak English as their first language, or if they are lacking practical access to internet-based solutions, you are potentially creating an information gap. There are ways around it for leaders who are dedicated to equity—a commitment to translating and printing out information that is being shared digitally and ensuring appropriate stakeholders groups receive the information can help. It takes more time, but so does equity.

Another challenge for digital tools is the skill set, technical confidence, and time associated with these tools. It can be challenging to learn a new tool, especially if a person is not particularly tech-savvy. Having a plan for new technology tools that includes up-front training and ongoing support is key. Giving people time during their work hours to learn a new tool is also critical. Bringing in a substitute for the day sends a message that the employee is valued—by the investment leaders are making in them in terms of time and training. Their attitude toward the new tool is likely to be much more positive in that environment.

Lastly, these tools are only as good as the quality of the content. Posting quality content in multiple ways through small tweaks is ideal, but every new tool involves at least some time investment. Educational leaders need to analyze the time investments they are currently making in their communication efforts and determine the strongest tools to invest their limited time based on reach and equity, not on what has always been done in the past. The checklist at the end of chapter 7 on social media has a number of questions to ask when considering a new tool.

ASK & ANSWER

- Have you conducted an audit of your communication channels?
- Have you developed a profile of your stakeholders? (Are they active on social media? Majority of iPhone users? Less tech savvy?)
- Based on the pros and cons, what are the best channels for your primary stakeholder audiences?
- Do your systems have the ability to translate to multiple languages?

EIGHT

Social Media

Dr. JoAnne Jackson, a veteran educator, has served as principal of Sturgess Middle School for more than sixteen years. She is known by her students, staff, and parents as a personable, hands-on, "old school" administrator whose leadership is well respected in the community. Her connections to business leaders, clergy, and local government officials are solid and they are great supporters of the school.

For years, Dr. Jackson successfully managed these networks with a communication style that relied heavily on personal connections and strong interpersonal relationships. When important messages needed to be communicated with parents, Dr. Jackson would send letters and flyers home with students. Urgent announcements were always sent via automated email and telephone messaging. Community partnerships were maintained through phone calls and monthly meetings; the school had little to no social media presence.

In March 2020, Sturgess Middle School joined school closures across the nation and shifted to remote learning as a result of the COVID-19 pandemic. In the months that followed, a barrage of information, guidelines, and recommendations for schools, from the Centers for Disease Control (CDC) to state and local public health departments, overwhelmed school systems. School administrators sought to ease the fears of parents even as they worked quickly to share information about their plans for remote learning, technology, grab 'n go lunches, and so on.

As the school struggled to keep up with disseminating the ever-changing flow of information, school and community stakeholders started to lose faith in Dr. Jackson's leadership. Her weekly messages were no longer viewed as timely or accurate, and the school's absence on social media led to rumors and conjecture within the online community. Parents soon became impatient with the lack of information and demanded daily updates and answers to their questions in real-time. For the first time, Dr. Jackson understood the value of using social media to *reach and respond to her school community. The pandemic laid bare the potential pitfalls of not engaging your school's stakeholders via online platforms. Today's social media culture demands that school administrators develop their school's online identity and then find ways to share and connect.*

SOCIAL MEDIA

Social media has changed the way school communities work, offering a new model to engage with families, staff, students, and the world at large. Like traditional media channels, it is a way to provide communication, but social media is unique in the way that people engage with an organization and the content that is posted. Social media at its core is social—it is a two-way communication channel that gives a voice to your district as well as your stakeholders. This two-way form of interaction can help a school to build stronger, more successful relationships. It also provides a way for the district to take part in important conversations that impact the school and the community.

There are a number of social media communication options, including the largest at the time of this book's publication—Twitter, Facebook, YouTube, LinkedIn, and Instagram. One of the most important steps in the four-step public relations process is research to determine which platform to use.

Research helps leaders to understand where their audience is and how to reach them. One the most important steps a school site can take is to ask their current and potential audiences/stakeholder groups about their communication activities and preferences. If a significant portion of the audience is on a social media platform, it is important that a school or department is there as well.

There are still some school leaders who would prefer to avoid social media. They are not confident in using it, fear online criticism, and they don't believe they have the time to take on one more thing. Perhaps they believe that if they don't have a social media presence that they can avoid the potentially negative online exchanges. Unfortunately, what happens is that the school or district is still discussed online on social media platforms, but without a presence, they lose the ability to provide information, correct misperceptions, or even just "listen" to the concerns.

One of the most significant implications of social media for schools is the expectation of accessibility and an immediate response. Whether it is a security concern, addressing a rumor, or providing event photos, students and families are expecting to receive information, updates, or a response immediately.

In fact, there are many cases in which an issue has gone "viral" and expanded into the national news before a district is able to respond.

Maintaining a social media presence increases the likelihood that your staff will know about an issue before the national news.

While it might seem like a lot to add one or two social media platforms to a school's communication tool belt, it is important to remember that leaders should be using the same messaging they use for other tools, with some adjustments for the platform. Rather than creating new content, schools should think of Twitter, Instagram, or Facebook as just one more tool. If there is a story or captioned photo you would already be posting to a website or next month's newsletter, push that same content out to your social media platforms as appropriate.

While it is tempting to think audiences might tire of seeing the same information in multiple places, the reality is that it can take several impressions (times that someone has seen a message) before they actually pay attention to it. Social media can help reinforce the information you are trying to get out in other ways.

In this book, we will cover the broad highlights of several tools, but for those wanting a more robust discussion of social media and how it can be done thoughtfully in schools, the book *The Social Media Imperative: School Leadership and Strategies for Success* by Kristin Magette is an authoritative resource on the topic.

FACEBOOK

Facebook is one of the most popular outlets for providing your stakeholders with regular information they will be interested in. While it is important to do your own research in case your community is different, the typical audiences for Facebook include family members, community organizations, and leaders. Students are not likely to be on Facebook until later in their lives and if they are on Facebook, they are not as active as their older counterparts.

Facebook's analytics are constantly changing. It is important to understand that just because your district makes a Facebook post, based on Facebook's own analytics, it will not be seen by all of your followers. Like most communication, Facebook posts are stronger when they include photos and videos. Even if it is a brief announcement, if it is provided in a graphic or colorful format, it is more likely to get the attention of the audience.

There are several monitoring options for alerts when a post is liked or shared, when the school's page is followed, and when a comment is made. Facebook offers robust internal analytics, and a representative of the school district should make a point of reviewing them on a regular basis to understand who is engaging with the school's page, when they are engaging, and the types of posts that increase engagement.

Facebook advertising (promoting a page or a post) can be extremely effective because of the precision it allows in targeting potential audiences. Facebook's Audience Insights helps leaders understand more about their current audience. It works by mining available data and showing exactly who your target market is, based on people who already like your page. Facebook also gives users the opportunity for social media managers to create ads using individual demographics, locations people have visited, interests, and behaviors to target people who do not currently follow a district's page.

INSTAGRAM

While Facebook is ideal for sharing information and content that quickly links back to your school's website, Instagram is ideal for sharing images of your students. At the time of this writing, Instagram has several options for sharing content with your followers. You can share photos and video content as a traditional post in your school's Instagram feed, posts as Stories that will disappear in twenty-four hours, longer videos in Instagram TV, or short fifteen-second video clips posted as Instagram Reels.

Instagram is owned by Facebook and the two share many of the same features. One of the greatest strengths of Instagram content is how easy it is to share content across other channels and platforms. Whether it's a quick picture at a school event or a photo you've scheduled to post in advance, a quick adjustment on your Instagram settings menu will automatically distribute that same content to your choice of Facebook, Twitter, Tumblr, Flickr, and other popular social media.

The typical Instagram audiences include students, some family members and more and more local businesses. The use of hashtags on photos and videos will help track your efforts as well as spread your messaging, helping it appear in front of anyone looking for content under your hashtag content area. Table 8.1 provides some ideas about weekly posts and associated hashtags for schools.

TWITTER

Twitter is a place where you can exhibit thought-leadership in education, family engagement, or other school-related topics with those who share similar interests, whether you know them or not. It's important to connect with/follow other organizations that might have content that your followers might find useful or informative. Following other Twitter accounts that relate to education and your district allows you to maintain a presence by sharing their content rather than coming up with new, original content all the time. It is also a great way to share active moments in

Table 8.1.

Day	Hashtag/Post
Monday	#MondayFunday: staff having fun at work #MondayMotivation: inspirational quotes to start the week off #MusicMonday: school music programs and events
Tuesday	#TransformationTuesday: a split before and after photo, great for showing progress over time #TipTuesday: share your knowledge and advice #TuesdayTreat: highlight a "treat" happening at a school—field trip, special event, etc.
Wednesday	#WayBackWednesday: historical photos and facts #WednesdayWisdom: famous quote to inspire or maybe one from a student
Thursday	#ThrowBackThursday: historical photos and facts #ThankfulThursday: gratitude for staff, families, community
Friday	#FridayNightFootball: ask them to post highlights and photos from the game #FridayFunday: similar to Monday Funday, show pics of your staff having fun, or it can be more open to sharing anything fun #FollowFriday: tag and highlight other organizations worth following #FlashBackFriday: similar to Throwback Thursday, follows the same theme of sharing old pics

your school—a photo or video with a brief comment about that day's lesson is a quick and easy way to promote your school program and staff.

Used widely, Twitter also makes it very easy to engage younger people and track your efforts through the use of hashtags related to your message. While there is a size limitation on Tweets, Twitter is perfect for sharing highlights and referring people to other platforms.

In addition to posting and reposting content on Twitter, a school district may want to invest in advertising on Twitter. There are different kinds of ads on Twitter, such as Promoted Tweets, Promoted Accounts, and Promoted Trends. You decide what you want to accomplish, for example attract more followers or persuade someone to visit a website. You can target your audience by the people they follow, their interests, behaviors, and demographics, the events they're interested in and even the pets they have. Please check the resources section of this book for additional articles about a variety of social media platforms.

LINKEDIN

While not thought of as traditional social media, LinkedIn has a place in digital branding that is similar. Your school will want to create and maintain a professional profile on LinkedIn to connect with current and potential employees and partners. You can network, share professional advice, and even recruit new talent. LinkedIn is about a network of professional colleagues and organizations, kind of like Facebook with a suit on.

It is a great place to post education-related content, introduce new initiatives from the business and community perspective, and engage on an industry level. Typical audiences include current and potential employees, foundation contributors, business partners, and community leaders. It is not as popular or heavily trafficked as other social media platforms, but like a website it is a great place to professionally represent your campus and staff.

A school leader might create and share blog posts about current education trends or special programs on their campus, job postings, events, or community partner information. You can view engagement metrics for organization updates (likes, comments, shares, and mentions) and receive notifications for different types of engagement.

Using the self-service LinkedIn Ads platform, you can create two types of ads: sponsored updates and text ads. Both of these allow you to send visitors to your website. The differences between the two are where they are displayed and how you create them. The cost of LinkedIn ads tends to run higher than other social platforms like Facebook and Twitter, but may be worth it to reach specific people for recruitment purposes.

Pros: Social media platforms are powerful communication channels because they are engaging, two-way, and meet people where they are already looking for and sharing information. Unless an organization wants to invest in paid advertising or scheduling tools, they are also very inexpensive compared with print or face-to-face channels. These platforms give an organization another avenue for responding to a crisis or anything that requires an immediate message.

Cons: The list of cons related to social media is similar to those encountered with any digital tool. There is a learning curve for new platforms, there are equity issues if you are not replicating the content elsewhere, and there is a limited amount of time in the day. The most important way to figure out if a social media platform is a good tool for a school is to find out if stakeholders are using it in numbers that justify the time investment.

QUESTIONS TO ASK WHEN CONSIDERING A NEW COMMUNICATION TOOL

General

- What will the new tool add to your communication and engagement efforts?

- Will it replace an existing channel or is it a completely new addition?
- Are there any district or state policies or regulations associated with the functionality of this platform?
- What are the potential risks associated with the use of this platform and how are you mitigating these risks?
- Whether or not a school plans to use a social media platform do you think you should claim your school or district's name on the platform?

Content Providers (People Writing the Posts)

- How many staff would have access to the platform as content providers?
- How many staff will be expected to post content on this platform?
- What is the learning curve for this platform?
- Will there be a review of posts by an administrator?

Audiences

- How many employees, families, or students currently use this platform?
- How many employees, families, or students would potentially use this platform?
- How do you know this?

Platform Content

- How often will you be posting using this platform?
- What kind of content will be posted on this platform?

Training

- How many users would need to be trained on the new platform?
- Is there training available?

Access

- Will the platform log in be set up so that district level and other administrators can get into the platform?
- Will the platform belong to the department or campus and be passed to the next leadership team?

Supplemental training materials available for this chapter at www.schoolprpro.com/the-communicating-principal.

NINE

Supportive Systems

Middle School Principal Meredith Neal had little time in the school day left after a lengthy meeting with her assistant principals. They had met to discuss increased behavior problems among the sixth and seventh graders during passing periods. The agreed-upon solution was to alter sixth grade schedules in an effort to limit co-mingling and ensure order in the hallways.

At the end of the school day, Principal Neal sent an email to her secretary, Ms. Busch, requesting that she use the school notification system to share information about the impending schedule change with parents.

As directed, the next morning, Ms. Busch crafted a seven-second message to all families. The typed message was inserted into the school notification system utilizing the text-to-speech option and read, "Dear Parents, please note that effective Monday, October 29th, all sixth grade students will begin a new schedule. Thank you." The message was set to begin broadcasting to all sixth, seventh, and eighth grade households at approximately 3:15 p.m., nearly one hour after dismissal.

The next morning, Principal Neal's office was inundated with calls from angry parents—many of whom did not have a sixth grade student—asking how the change would affect their seventh and eighth graders. Other parents anxiously inquired as to whether or not the changing schedule would impact school bus routes. Some expressed frustration at not being able to find any additional information on the school's website.

Naturally, as more parents took to social media to discuss the issue, speculation gave rise to rumors about the "real reason" for the school's decision. By the end of the week, Principal Neal was compelled to issue a school-wide letter of apology to all middle school families for the confusion caused by the message.

Despite the many "hats" that must be worn by school leaders, helping staff understand how to effectively utilize system tools is a necessary skill that can either enhance community trust or create a fog of confusion.

Rightfully, Ms. Busch acted as a tactician by sending the message out to parents as directed by Principal Neal. However, it was the lack of an established system for sending out that type of message that led to the miscommunication. Think about what caused this confusion and potential systems that could have been in place to prevent it. With training, key members of the team such as school secretaries, clerks, and even volunteers can become vital partners in leveraging the impact of effective school communication.

With all that is included in this book about communications on your campus or in your district, you might wonder where you will find the time to tackle a second job. Yes, communicating effectively takes work. However, it will also lessen the load in a number of other areas. Good communication can lessen the time a leader spends dealing with complaints, reacting to real or imagined crises, recruiting new employees, and promoting the strengths of the school or program.

How does that happen? When a leader creates simple systems that work within a given environment (considering the strengths and assets, time, volunteers, culture), the result is that communication can be exponentially improved with a little upfront investment and limited ongoing maintenance.

Systems bring all that you have to work with together and create a synergy that multiplies the effort you put into them. For example, if someone writes a short website message about an upcoming school break to remind families and staff, that might take an initial investment of thirty minutes, especially if previous messages have been saved to be reused later. If there is a system in place that automatically reposts that message in social media feeds, an email, and any other primary channels, that initial investment that might have reached the small number of people actively looking for information now reaches people who are simply scrolling through their Facebook feed.

That kind of system can be set up through an IFTTT (If this, then that) code between multiple applications or even an online message scheduling tool. Sounds great for leaders who are technologically savvy, but there are also plenty of low-tech solutions that can help make communication efforts more powerful.

COMMUNICATION OPTIONS WORKSHEET

One easy-to-implement system involves a worksheet that documents the communication channels in your school, the audiences those channels reach, and additional columns to increase clarity and accountability.

The first step, of course, is conducting research to confirm the strongest communication options that are currently being used and discover additional options audiences would like to see implemented. While it is important for audiences to know consistently where to look for information—for example, a school's website or Facebook page, it is also important to reach out to new potential audiences using the same platforms they are already using. It is similar to what many teachers subscribe to in the classroom, "meeting people where they are."

When asking audiences about current communication methods, it is important to ask it in at least two questions—one that documents the ways a respondent has received information and a second question to determine how effective each communication method has been for them.

Why two questions? There could be an existing communication method, for example, a printed school newsletter, that might be one way that families know they can find information. However, it could also be a tool that they find cumbersome—it can be easily lost, it takes a lot of time to find specific pieces of information within the newsletter, and there is a delay in how quickly the information can be shared.

The first question should include phrasing similar to, "Please select each of the ways you have received information about our schools and programs" and include a drop-down menu or checklist of communication methods. Providing this question in a quantitative format achieves two goals: it makes it much easier to analyze the responses and it informs respondents about the variety of communication methods currently available.

The second question might be something like, "Please rate the effectiveness of our communication tools." The question would list the same communication tools that were included in the first and have a simple scale of 1=Not Very Effective to 5=Very Effective to allow respondents to rate them. It is also helpful to ask respondents to skip and not rate the methods they haven't used.

Discovering new potential communication tools suggested by respondents requires a different type of question. Unless the survey writer is very certain about the tools that might be suggested, the question should be open-ended. For example, it might read, "Are there any specific communication tools you think we should be using?"

This type of open-ended question will likely confirm some of the ideas a leader already had about new platforms, but it might also suggest tools they hadn't known about or considered. In the case of suggested tools, it is important to understand how representative the suggestion might be. Introducing a new platform is work and it requires an ongoing commitment of time. Unless it is overwhelmingly obvious based on the survey results, it might be a good idea to confirm the results using a question on a survey or poll and listing just that tool to determine how many audience members are using it.

It is very important that as you review the tools you will include on this sheet that you consider how accessible these tools may be to certain members of your stakeholder community. For example, if you have mostly digital methods of communication on the sheet but a percentage of your families or community members don't access digital content often enough, they will not receive information equitably and both the school system and family could suffer as a result.

Once your communication tool list is complete, you can put together your worksheet. Start with an area at the top of the worksheet for the issue that needs to be communicated. Then create a table that includes the list of the tools in the left column and add a column for the audiences that receive information through that tool, another for who is responsible for communicating using that tool, what the deadline is for communicating out using that tool, and lastly one for marking when that communication is completed. See the communication options sample on the supplemental website www.schoolprpro.com/the-communicating-principal for inspiration. Depending on how savvy a leader is with technology, the worksheet could be created on paper or a spreadsheet program like Google Sheets or Microsoft Excel.

The worksheet can be used in a variety of ways to save time and organize communication efforts. For example, in a meeting where an issue comes up that needs a mini communication plan, the sheet can provide the variety of tools available along with the primary audiences they reach so that meeting attendees don't have to brainstorm these methods each time they need to communicate something out.

In addition, the sheets provide a structure for organizing and tracking communication efforts. At subsequent meetings, the sheets can be used to check on the implementation and follow through on each of the items.

As communication efforts are being documented on these sheets, a sizable amount of data will be collected about issues and communication tools. This is great data to be shared with internal audiences like district leaders as well as outside leaders like families and community members. This kind of data helps make explicit the effort that is undertaken to communicate effectively.

REPURPOSING CONTENT

Developing an effective message takes time. Who is the audience, where are they on the issue? What do they need to know about the issue? The first time a message is developed is an investment. Developing a system to make the most of the content involves modifying the initial messaging to be appropriate for a slightly different audience and tool.

A message for a website can be longer than other platforms and include several photos and links to other content or sites. It also must be written for a general audience and include information that would be useful for a variety of stakeholders. On the other hand, that same message would need to be adjusted for a school's Twitter account.

It would need to be much shorter to meet the platform's character count. It might also need to be modified to meet the school's tone on Twitter. While a website might have a general/professional tone, schools should sound more like an individual on their social media platforms, taking the opportunities to root for students and staff, grieve with them, and when comfortable joke with them. Read more about reducing, reusing, and recycling content in chapter 6 on messaging.

FEEDBACK LOOP

Another systemic habit that greatly benefits schools is to always consider how you are collecting feedback as part of a communication effort. For example, are you considering additional questions that may come up as a result of the message? Where can people go for additional information about a given topic? Including links to email addresses, phone numbers, and websites within the school system or resources outside the system are a great way to support your audiences' interest in more information. It may even cut down on the amount of follow-up communication needed.

Collecting feedback about the issue is a great way to understand where your audience(s) stands on the issue as well as the language that they are using around the issue. A Sacramento area school district learned that when they launched an open-ended question about their efforts to build upon their career technical programs.

One of the replies was very telling. It read something along the lines of, "I don't care about all of this stuff, I want to hear more about ROP programs." It became apparent to the district that they needed to include additional explanatory language that made it clear the two were one in the same. This is the kind of insight that dramatically improves the ability of messages to connect with the people they are intended to reach.

Feedback opportunities are also a great way to track communication efforts. If a link is included in a social media ad or e-newsletter, often there is an automatic report generated that can tell a leader how many people took the next step when they read the message. If there are certain links that are receiving more interest than others, that's valuable data that can help drive future communication efforts.

BUILDING CAPACITY

Even if a leader is convinced of the importance of effective communication at their campus, that doesn't mean they have the extra time for it. A principal's time is premium. They are responsible for overseeing everything that happens on campus—from classroom schedules to the drop-off process to the playground supervision and much more.

Developing an effective system for delegating the creation of content is one way that communication efforts can be expanded without a lot of extra time. There are likely a number of people involved in the school or district that have an interest in helping get the word out about the positive things that are happening.

For example, high school administrators have provided the opportunity for students to assist with content creation as part of a class or club, giving them an opportunity to have real-world experience along with promoting their campus. Other school leaders have allowed Parent Teacher Association officers or other volunteers to assist.

There may also be teachers or other staff that are willing to jump in to help. Taking on the additional responsibility could be rewarded with a stipend, lessened workload, or if neither of those is possible, gift cards and equipment like a high-tech phone or camera.

There is probably some concern and reluctance to delegate such an important responsibility and it shouldn't be done casually. There are a number of ways a leader can ensure that the content that gets distributed meets their standards and upholds the campus brand. One is to create a system of review before the content is released to the public. Reviewing is still going to take up a certain amount of time, so that might also be something that can be delegated to a trusted staff member after a certain period of time.

When building capacity, please keep in mind a couple of ways to ensure that your communication is as representative as possible. When offering up the opportunity to assist with communication, be careful not to limit the announcement of that opportunity to only people or groups you feel comfortable with. There may be people outside of your trusted group that could offer invaluable insight into your messages that help them reach people who are not like you or most of your staff.

ASK & ANSWER

- Do you have a list of the available communication options at your school handy so that you can easily brainstorm your communication options?
- How can others at your school assist with communicating?
- How can you reuse the same content in multiple ways in your communication efforts?

TEN

Crisis Communication

Greenwicke Elementary School's principal Jordan Roberts expected dismissal time on the last day of school before spring break to be typical—managed mayhem—as excited students ran toward their busses and waved goodbye to their teachers and other support staff.

More than a half-hour after dismissal, her day would take an unexpected turn after her secretary forwarded her a frantic call from a parent stating that her second-grader never made it home.

As a veteran administrator, Principal Roberts prided herself on always being prepared for whatever crisis might come her way. Armed with her emergency contact list, she immediately called the local police department to report the student missing. Next, she directed her secretary to check the student information system to confirm the student's attendance for the day as she spoke to school bus officials about the student's bus route.

Fortunately, a short time later, a call from the bus company revealed they had safely located the student who had fallen asleep on the bus and missed his stop. The school bus driver neglected to sweep the bus before exiting and hadn't noticed the student sleeping in the back seat.

Principal Roberts quickly drafted an automated message to all of her parents, alerting them to the incident. She understood that families of lower grade students would be particularly interested in knowing that the student was safe. Despite the bus company's stated liability for the mishap, Principal Roberts was also aware that, at that moment, families wanted to know that someone was managing the crisis. It was also critical that they hear the school's plan to keep their children safe. This particular crisis required her to analyze the situation, understand what safeguards were needed, and create a common-sense solution.

As news of the incident began circulating on social media, Principal Roberts took to Facebook to respond to questions about the incident to manage the narrative and reduce the likelihood of rumor and misinformation. The platform also

81

allowed her to "get ahead" of the crisis by sharing her new, proactive Five-Point Plan for school bus safety to prevent future incidents. Rather than simply blame the school bus company, Principal Roberts assured families that she would be responsible for monitoring its adherence to the plan. Her diligent response ultimately renewed their trust in her leadership.

COMMUNICATING IN A CRISIS

There are a variety of crises that can impact a school, each of them uniquely challenging. Schools are one of the places where things are expected to go perfectly. Every day, the buses should run on time, the schools should be safe places with kind teachers and engaging activities. Students expect be challenged, respected, and protected. Leaders should be wise, open, and communicate just the right thing at just the right time.

When a campus or system falls short, stakeholder groups will be disappointed. However, if a school leader and system respond well, this can actually improve the perception of the campus and its staff.

There are three primary crises that afflict schools: physical emergencies, individual incidents, and crises of confidence.

Physical emergencies are those things that physically affect the campus, students, and staff. A fire on the playground, non-working air conditioning units, or an outbreak of a disease on campus are all examples of the kinds of physical emergencies a leader will be called upon to respond to.

Individual incidents occur when someone in the system is caught or perceived to be behaving badly. A teacher shows up to school intoxicated, the Parent-Teacher Association (PTA) president steals the funds set aside for a field trip, or a support staff member arrest are all examples.

Crises of confidence are the most difficult challenges to address because the leader or system has lost credibility with stakeholders. It occurs when there has been some kind of failure in the system that leads to a loss of trust. An example might be when an employee does something wrong, but remains in a position that places them with children or when a school leader makes a big decision without the input of the people who would be impacted by it. It takes a lot more effort to respond to this third type of crisis because the trust has to be slowly rebuilt and there is no room for mistakes.

Regardless of the type of crisis, there is a four-step public relations process that can be applied to ensure that good decisions are being made and communicated. The first step is research. As soon as you are made aware of an issue, work quickly to collect reliable information about it. Find out who was involved, what specifically happened at what time and where. When possible, confirm that information with more than one person. Most importantly, don't speculate about the answers.

The second step is planning. Once you have collected all the relevant details and confirmed them, decide which facts can be shared, who needs to know them, and in what order they should be told. Some of the information you collect may not be shareable because of privacy regulations or an ongoing investigation.

Deciding who needs to know the remaining information and in what order they should be informed is important. If a group feels disrespected because they were left without information, your lack of communication could become part of the crisis and further deteriorate trust.

In most cases, you want to take an inside-out approach to communicating, especially in a crisis. Families and staff will not appreciate hearing about a school-related crisis from the media or a Facebook—they want to hear from you. Think of it like ripples in a pond when a rock is thrown into it. Those at the center of the ripple are those immediately impacted by the situation. For example, the students and staff who have been teaching and learning in a classroom that has toxic mold.

The third step is implementation, that is, the crafting of messages to convey the information that can be shared. Messaging is not just about providing information, but understanding the audience and providing it in a way that addresses their needs. For example, when a school is being closed, the information needed for the staff who work there, the families of the students that attend there, and the neighbors to the property are very different. Also consider the timing of messaging. In a physical crisis especially, it is critical to work fast to get information out.

Two of the most valuable messaging formats in a crisis are draft statements and speaking points. The statement can be posted on all digital channels, sent out to media or stakeholder inquiries, and tweaked to serve as an email notification. Speaking points are focused on key messages you hope will resonate with audiences and are usually drafted as bulleted phrases under key topic areas. They are helpful for anyone that interacts with stakeholders (e.g., office staff, board members, teachers) so that they have general language that they can modify to their communication style. This helps to ensure messages are consistent. To see a sample of key messages and speaking points, visit https://www.schoolprpro.com/the-communicating-principal.

One way to start creating these messages is to start with a list of audiences and brainstorm the key issues related to each. Some will have shared interested and key issues and some will be unique to that audience. Create a master document of all the key issues and go through them one by one to identify responses and supporting material where appropriate.

For example, in dealing with a school closure, the issue of utilization of that property use will be a key issue for neighbors. Under that issue, a school leader might note that there are still a number of options under consideration for the property—an additional community library, a per-

forming arts school, or the new hub for district maintenance and operations. There are also a number of ways for neighbors to weigh in on the
decision—school board meetings, surveys, and a specialized email address for input. You might include all of these elements on a master
document for easy access.

Once the master document is compiled, the statements and speaking
points can be crafted using the same language in multiple places. For
example, Facebook, Twitter, the website, an email, and an automated call.
This will cut down on the amount of time it takes to craft the messages,
and ensure message discipline and consistency across audiences and
platforms.

While developing the messages, it is important to bring in representative advisors who can help craft, review, and make suggestions about
what will work for different audiences. Bring them in again when it
comes to the fourth step, evaluating the crisis response. Although it may
feel like the last thing anyone wants to do, revisiting the way the crisis
unfolded and identifying without blame how the response could have
been better will help everyone involved grow in this area.

In addition, considering the following five areas will help guide crisis
communicators toward the right messaging and tone. They include remaining on the right side of the issue, standing between both worlds,
thinking long-term, staying student-centered, and understanding the
larger context.

DON'T GET DEFENSIVE

It is natural to begin to feel loyalty to a school or system after working
there for some time. Schools are amazing places, and educators and support staff are some of the best people out there. However, when an issue
comes up, it is important to reflect on where our bias toward an institu-
tion might cloud our response.

Unfortunately, when school leaders are confronted with an issue and
immediately feel defensive about it, they often fall into the precarious
position of defending bad behavior or bad policy. That is more likely to
happen when the issue is raised by someone unknown to us or is presented in such a way that we feel attacked.

When the most critical parent at the school calls to report a problem
with a teacher who is well-liked by their peers, it is human nature to side
with the teacher. However, it is not until a claim has been researched that
we know its validity. Bias toward peers, school, and system can blind
leaders to real issues that affect student wellness and learning.

STAND BETWEEN BOTH WORLDS

When in a leadership position, it is natural to believe that you represent the best interests of the organization. However, leading a school means taking on a responsibility to manage a community-based resource. Your campus has been funded and supported by the area families and taxpayers and they should be represented in your thinking.

It is important to maintain a perspective that reflects the dual responsibility to district leadership and the students, staff, families, and community. When a crisis hits, thinking about the issue from the perspectives of the variety of all stakeholders served will make the messaging more effective.

THINK LONG-TERM

When considering the messages in response to a crisis it is important to think about your response and how it will impact stakeholders today and in the future. For example, when the teacher's union has made an exaggerated complaint around working conditions at a campus, it can be tempting to "hit back" at the union.

It may feel good in the moment to attack the group that is attacking the campus, but it doesn't serve either party in the long-term. While it may feel like a righteous battle, to everyone on the outside, it appears to be petty infighting at best and unprofessional at worst. It's important to always keep the long-term interests of the school community in mind. In this example, that interest is in keeping the respect of stakeholders for leaders and teachers.

STUDENT-CENTERED

Most importantly, the greatest test of messaging is to ask how it references student needs. At the heart of how every issue should be addressing the needs of the most important stakeholders in the system—students. Are they physically and mentally safe? What resources are available for them? What adjustments are being made to serve them better?

As a leader is putting together the list of items needed to address in a crisis response, the first question to ask is, "How does this affect students?" It is also an important question to ask in reviewing potential statements and speaking points. Taking care of staff is connected to taking care of students. When we remove the obstacles to teaching, we do that not just to make life better for teachers, but also to ensure there is the mental space and energy for teachers to better serve students. Don't assume that people understand that; make that connection explicit.

CONTEXT

Beyond the long-term, it is important to think about the broader context of the issue. Is this the first time anything like this has happened? Does it connect with anything that is currently happening on a regional or national level? Who is impacted by the issue and what groups are they associated with? What are the social and political implications around this issue?

While the answer to these questions may not impact how a leader responds to an issue, it can help guide the tone of the messaging and keep leaders aware of the interconnected issues at play. It can also illuminate potential situations that may come up in the days and weeks after the immediate crisis.

FOUR R'S OF CRISIS COMMUNICATION

Another system that can help guide and effective crisis response is to keep in mind the four R's—the Roles, Relationships, and Resources that equal an organization's Reputation. When a leader invests in the roles, relationships, and resources before and during a crisis, that organization will fare infinitely better than one that does not.

Roles

The day a crisis emerges is not the optimal time to begin the discussion about roles. Crisis planning should include a discussion about who is doing what when a crisis arises. One of those roles should be a point person for collecting information, and another is someone who can speak for the school or district. Ideally, these are two different people because in an intense crisis situation, the demand on both ends will be enormous.

If possible, identify a third person to confirm the information that is coming in. Create a document or physical whiteboard with two columns—on one side include new information coming in and on the other side, include the time and name of someone confirming the information. While it is not always possible to take this extra step, it does ensure that the information released is accurate and builds long-term credibility.

Leaders who take the time to confirm information before putting it out may face short-term criticism. Reporters and social media followers may point out that other people or organizations are stating something that you are not yet sure is true. The best response is to explain that you can appreciate the demand for information as quickly as possible but that you're committed to ensuring that anything your organization releases is accurate and can be trusted. These initial statements are referred to as holding statements.

While each of these communication roles is important, there is another that often gets overlooked. While people are working in the middle of the crisis, don't forget to assign someone to take care of others. That means making sure people are eating, that they are drinking water, that they are getting up and walking around every now and then and that when needed, they are advised to get rest.

This may seem like a luxurious unnecessary role, but a crisis response requires us to be at our best. Mistakes in a crisis are amplified and can be damaging on a variety of levels. Taking care of the people that need to have their full focus on the tasks at hand is not only smart, it's critical.

Relationships

This is another area that needs attention well before a crisis hits. Relationships with area agencies, with a variety of stakeholder groups and with the local media can be lifesavers when the stakes are high.

Build your personal relational capital with a variety of stakeholder groups, and be sure to include the people who are usually critics. One of the most important ways to do this is with honesty and transparency, especially about challenges.

It may seem counterintuitive to share vulnerable things with the people that have been critical, but that is the first step to building trust. Once they know that you have been honest about smaller difficult things, they are more likely to give you the benefit of the doubt when a crisis comes along.

Make time to support neighboring agencies. Being a school leader is one of the most intense jobs on the planet and there is always something else you could be doing. At the end of the day, the last thing you might want to do is attend the local Lions Club Rodeo to be a judge, but those are the times you are investing in relationships that will help your school and students in the long run.

The vulnerability in being transparent about less than impressive things, and the time spent attending meetings and representing the school or district in the community is like pouring water into a trust bucket. Little by little, action by action, that bucket eventually fills. When a crisis arises, especially through a leadership failure, some of that trust will be used. If you have an empty bucket, it is far more difficult.

Resources

Another area in which leaders can prepare for a crisis is in collecting a variety of communication resources. Just like someone might have a Go Bag of emergency supplies in their home, school leaders should be prepared for the next communication crisis with a variety of templates and lists in digital and print formats.

One way to do this is to pay attention to the way that colleagues and other leaders respond publicly in a crisis situation. Copy those messages that you feel are effective and place them in a folder organized by theme, for example, messages about closing the school for a physical emergency or messages about the bad behavior of a staff person. In a crisis situation, you'll be able to quickly pull up a message that can be modified to fit the right audiences and situation.

In addition to messaging, keep a list of area resources that can be helpful in an emergency situation. People with area utility companies, local government agencies, nonprofit groups, advocacy groups, and faith leaders are all great resources for schools and another reason to spend time connecting in the community.

Your Reaction Equals Your Reputation

Having the roles defined and practiced and the resources identified and ready are a great foundation for crisis communication planning. A humble, caring, and transparent response is the building we place on that foundation.

If you've followed the four-step public relations process, you've done your research on the issue and confirmed the problem. If it is something that happened as a result of a failure in your system (people, policy, or practice), own it. Leaders who fail to do that have already lost a large part of the audience that is hungry for authenticity.

Once you've explained the problem, communicate the solution. What are you doing about it now? How will you keep it from happening again? The immediate actions include what your campus is doing to keep students and staff safe and meet urgent needs.

Longer term, look to the cause of the issue and propose a different path forward. If you do not yet know what will be changing, let your stakeholders know that you understand change is needed and you are working on it and will consult with stakeholders. Some will not believe you—they will wait to see if you follow through on your promises. Include a time period for action and change and meet it.

In the middle of a crisis, it is more important than ever that leaders are communicating well and often. Even if there has been no change in the information known or the circumstances, reach out to stakeholders and let them know what you're working on and that you are still focused on the issue.

During the middle of 2020 and the COVID-19 pandemic, when many schools were in a long-term online learning situation, not a lot was changing on a day-to-day basis. However, receiving weekly messages from principals and other leaders helped students, staff, and families feel more connected even when they couldn't be in person.

The tone of the messaging is also important. So many in education have been trained to be the experts in the room and speak in professional, academic language. In a crisis, it is critical to humanize the school and show appropriate emotion. Even if the crisis was not caused by a failure in the system, recognize the challenging experience that people are going through.

PREVENTABLE CRISIS

While there are some crises that will happen no matter what a leader does, there are a lot that can be avoided by staying true to your values as an educational leader. In the classroom, we often tout our high expectations—those should be applied to all who are part of the school community, not just students. Holding everyone accountable is not easy work, but it ensures that the people that remain employed in schools are worthy of the role.

That accountability must extend all the way to the top, with ethical and fiscally responsible actions and policies. It is said that to really know an organization or a household, look at how they spend their money. Does the school or district budget reflect the organizational values? Do leaders profess to care about things like diversity and yet have no funds set aside for recruitment of more employees of color? The gap between what is said and what is done erodes trust and is ripe for a crisis of confidence.

Caring and connected leaders and staff are the antidote to distrust. Beyond meeting the basic requirements of the job, healthy and collaborative cultures foster employees that feel valued and conduct themselves in a way that builds a tight community of stakeholders.

Lastly, the openness, responsiveness, and transparency of the organization can help with avoiding a crisis. When a leader is open and approachable, they are far more likely to hear about small issues early on before they grow into a bigger problems. When they are responsive and transparent, stakeholders trust that they will do what is needed to address the situation and are less likely to escalate the issue to get the needed attention.

It really comes down to doing the right thing as a leader. Yes, leadership requires compromise, but values are never negotiable. Even if a leader's response to a crisis isn't perfect, their ongoing commitment to the campus and investment in stakeholder relationships will buffer any small missteps and ensure they receive the benefit of the doubt from the people paying attention.

ASK & ANSWER

- Have you developed a checklist of important phone numbers and contacts in the event of a crisis?
- Before drafting or making any statement in response to the crisis, have you verified your information as fact?
- Have you identified a trusted advisor to check your communication for tone?

Supplemental training materials available for this chapter at www.schoolprpro.com/the-communicating-principal.

ELEVEN

Working with the Media

If there's one thing middle school assistant principal Reggie Henson worked hard his entire career to avoid, it was the media. Naturally, much of his work involved student discipline and oversight of the school's dean's office—the least of which offered much in the way of what the public would consider "good news." Assistant Principal Henson quietly assumed a role under the radar and kept his fingers crossed that no errant student behaviors would result in a call from the media.

Recently, he had been dealing with a rash of fights that was compounded by students videotaping and posting them on social media. In response, he began the rollout of the district's new Restorative Justice Program which empowers students to resolve their conflicts in small groups called Peace Circles. As parents began contacting him about the viral videos, he knew that it was only a matter of time before the press would follow up on the story.

While the program had yet to yield any immediate success, there were a couple of instances where students who participated in the Peace Circles showed a reduction in fights at school. In an administrator's meeting with his principal, Assistant Principal Henson shared his concern about the fights and viral videos being circulated on social media.

"Why don't you contact the media yourself?" Principal Thompson asked to his astonishment. Not sure he'd heard him correctly he responded slowly, "Call and tell them that we have fights that have gone viral?" Assistant Principal Henson asked. "No," Principal Thompson said, "call and tell them what we're doing about it."

As they continued to brainstorm and analyze data related to the new Restorative Justice Program, Assistant Principal Henson grew less anxious about reaching out to the media. He began to feel excitement at the chance to bring attention to the benefits of the new initiative. Moreover, he was relieved that the middle school would be able to tell its own story by being transparent about the issue and providing real-life examples, research, and discipline data.

The following week, Assistant Principal Henson invited a local news reporter to attend one of the school's Peace Circles to view the program in action. With permission from parents, the reporter interviewed several students who answered questions about how the restorative model was helping them manage their personal conflicts with other students and at home.

The story ran locally and was added to the school's website and posted to the district's social media platforms. Overall, there was a tremendous outpouring of support from parents and community members, as well as interest from neighboring school districts inquiring about how to start a Restorative Justice Program at their schools.

The media landscape has changed dramatically over the past three decades. There have been intense rounds of employee layoffs, consolidations of smaller outlets into larger conglomerates, and increased competition from decentralized and informal sources of information.

With fewer specialized reporters in education and the rush to get information out before it is out on blogs and social media, there is arguably less time and effort spent on issues. That makes it even more important for school leaders to educate reporters and editors about complex educational issues—prior to and during a story.

In addition to the industry changes, there have been dramatic adjustments in media viewership. Since 2004, Pew Research Center has issued an annual report on the U.S. news media industry. During that time, the viewing trends for local media have been falling, especially for younger audiences. As leaders are thinking about the best investment of energy and effort for promoting their school or campus, understanding if the intended audiences will be reached through local media is a strong consideration.

RESPONDING TO THE MEDIA

If responding to a media inquiry about your school or district, keep in mind that they may not fully understand the issue they are calling about. They receive a call from someone and decide to call the campus to check it out—that may be as much background as they've been given. They have in their mind what the story is likely to be, but it's your job to let them know the full story.

Think of the issue or potential story as a whole pie. Reporters only see the slice that they've been given. It's up to the school leader to talk with them and help them see the bigger picture. Your goal is to make sure they file a full and fair story, not just answer questions about their story narrative.

Even though there is a great deal of turnover in media outlets, when possible try to build relationships with local reporters. Invite them to newsworthy activities and events so that they become familiar with your school and so that the first contact you have with them isn't an intense media story.

When they do call for your response to a potentially negative story, don't be afraid to interview them. Ask them what they know about the story so far and whom they have talked to about it. Many if not most will be happy to share that information with you if you are asking in a friendly and respectful way. If you don't have immediate access to the information they are asking for or need time to confirm what they say they've uncovered about an issue, let them know that. Provide a time when you will respond, and meet that time—even if you do not yet have answers, be in touch to let them know that and set a time when you believe you will.

Never, ever lie to a reporter. It is a surefire way to become the story. Be honest about the issues and address them head-on, even when they are negative. In the short term it can be tough to take the media hit on something you did wrong as a leader or system. However, you are far more likely to win the respect of the reporter and public if you are honest up front.

Remember that your role is not just to respond to the questions the reporter provides, but to also add context. Provide background when possible so that they get a better perspective on the complexity of the issues involved. If you know and trust the reporter, you can provide that information as "background" so that it is not attributed to you personally.

MEDIA OUTREACH

If you want to use the media as a channel for promoting your school or program, start with some research about the best outlets and individuals to contact. If it is a human interest story, don't attempt to contact the investigative reporter. If there are some stations and papers that tend to cover education, they might be at the top of your list for outreach.

Once you've developed the list of people you plan to contact about the story, put together your media "pitch" and make it unique to each person. Read and compliment them on recent stories, express appreciation for their focus on certain issues. Let them know that you're aware of their work and not just sending the same message out to everyone.

NEWSWORTHINESS

Even the best written pitch is not going to result in media coverage if the issue or event doesn't rise to the level of newsworthy. Unfortunately, simply providing a good product or service isn't news because it is what is expected to happen. Not providing a good product or service, however, is news.

Many school administrators get very frustrated with the media, and feel they or their schools are being unfairly targeted because it seems only the negative things are covered. But reporters cover things that are different, new, controversial, and spark public response. They do not generally cover the things that are expected and ongoing.

There are several areas of newsworthiness that can appeal to a reporter, and when making a pitch to get a story or event covered, it can be helpful to connect one or more of these:

- Immediacy: the story or event should be about to happen or just happened. Unfortunately, if your students conducted a project that ended a week ago, it would lose the newness that makes it feel like news.
- Proximity: we care about what happens in our area, so those things that take place in the immediate region are of interest. Trying to get a station in a different media market to care about your story is more challenging because they want to cover stories their viewers care about.
- Human interest: people care about people so stories that show passion, inspiration, and triumph over tremendous challenges are also newsworthy.
- Currency: does the story tie in with something happening at a national level or throughout several areas at this time? For example, do you have a student that created a budgeting tool while Congress is debating the national debt?
- Prominence: do you have a famous alumnus who will be coming back for a visit at the campus and talking with students? Well-known people who are associated with a story make it newsworthy.
- Impact: how many people will be affected by the issue and in what way? The larger the impact, the more interesting the story.
- Novelty: Is this the first time that something has happened? Is it a one-of-a-kind event or story?
- Conflict: when something is dramatic in nature, it creates general interest.

Once you've decided the story you want to pitch is newsworthy, it is time to reach out and contact the reporter. Based your research on the reporter and outlet and/or your experience with them, communicate with each reporter based on their preference. Some like to receive an email, others are less formal and would be happy to receive a text or even a Twitter direct message.

The important thing is that your communication to them is both targeted and relevant. Comment on a previous similar story they wrote.

Explain why your story is important for their specific audience (news value). Your pitch should sound like it was written specifically for them because it was.

Keep in mind that even if it is a worthwhile story, it still may not rise to the level of being covered. At any given time, there are always many different potential news stories underway. A reporter could have agreed to cover the event, but something more dramatic or impactful could take precedent. Don't be too upset, just reach out again the next time you have something that might work.

BE READY

If the reporter agrees to cover your story, you have more work to do. Rather than just let the story evolve, proactively decide that your objective is for the story—What do you want people to know and remember about it?

Develop a few key messages, don't try to cram so much into an interview that it is difficult to tell what is important. Key messages are the important things you want people to understand about the situation and it is usually less than five items. For example, in an interview about having to cut a program, your key messages might include information about the budget cuts everyone is facing, the feedback you solicited from stakeholders about their priorities, and how many other programs will still be offered, especially if they are similar. Remember your reporter may not have much background with the issue so show them what is important to cover by focusing on a few strong points.

Once you've decided on your key messages, develop a couple talking points under each one to illustrate them. This could include data that backs up the message, a story about specific people affected or involved, or an analogy that makes for a good sound bite.

As the reporter is asking you about the issue, be responsive but also try to stay "on message" as much as possible. The way to do this is to lead the conversation back to your main points. Some sample phrases that can help include:

- It's important to know . . .
- The larger issue is . . .
- Our top priority is . . .
- It is critical that people understand . . .
- We need to remember that . . .
- Our main concern is that . . .
- Let's not lose sight of the underlying issue . . .

The wording that you use in your interview is also important. Be as concise as possible because the story itself will be a fraction of the interview and you don't want to rely on the reporter to decide what is important. Avoid bureaucratic language and acronyms as much as possible, using layperson language and everyday analogies when possible.

The easier it is for people to relate to what you are saying, the more likely that soundbite will actually make it into the story. Soundbites are short pieces of your interview that are utilized in the piece. For example, "Cleaning a house with a toddler is like brushing your teeth while eating Oreos" is a sound bite that most parents can relate to. They should be crafted as supporting material for your key messages.

When crafting soundbite language, make sure you run it past several people to ensure that it is appropriate to the issue and not offensive. Soundbites work because they are relatable, but they are also extremely contextual—what is relatable to some may not work for others.

The language you use to describe your school and programs should be personal and warm. Try to avoid internal terms that make you sound like a bureaucrat. For example, "Students with special needs are welcome in our exciting science and engineering pathways" sounds much better than "Pupils with IEPs are allowed to take STEM courses."

NO COMMENT

There will be times when it will be impossible to answer a question from the media. For example, there may be some kind of legal confidentiality, it may be premature to guess about what might unfold, there may be privacy protections in place for students or staff, or there could be the potential for litigation.

However, just because you can't answer the specific question that was asked, doesn't mean that you have to reply, "No comment." There are a number of no comment alternatives that will allow you to provide the interviewer and their audience with more context and place you and your organization in a better light. A few examples are listed below.

- I would very much like to comment on this issue, but unfortunately state law [name the code and number] requires [and explain in layperson's terms].
- I can't comment on this specific case, but what I can say is . . . [and explain how your district policy would dictate how to handle a case just like this].
- I don't have all the facts to be able to answer that question accurately but I can tell you that . . . [explain what you do know and what you are doing to support students and staff].
- It is premature to discuss that because we have not yet confirmed the details

- That is a hypothetical question I can't answer, but I would be happy to talk about what we are doing to support students and staff while the situation evolves.
- I know you would like more information, but we are legally responsible to protect the privacy of our staff.

THE MESSENGER

In addition to the key messages and soundbites that you prepare ahead of time, the person who conducts the interview also sends a message. Who is the person in your organization most closely aligned with the issue? If it is a story about providing homeless students with supplies, perhaps the school social worker is the best fit. They will be able to speak from personal experience and provide relatable examples in support of the key messages.

Beyond the issue, there may be additional context that needs to be considered. If the school is partnering with a prominent local church, perhaps the well-known pastor should be the person conducting the interview. This lends credibility and sends an underlying message of partnership and investment with the community.

Lastly, consider the skill level of the potential interviewee. While it is ideal if the person is connected to the issue, if they are nervous to the point of panic, they will not be able to confidently represent the school or the program.

When the spokesperson is selected, ensure that they know the key messages and if it is potentially a controversial topic, make sure that they prepare for the worst-case questions. Practicing with a colleague can be very helpful, but don't focus on saying the exact answer each time, rather keep the key messages in mind and answer in an authentic way, supported by data, stories, and analogies.

If it has the possibility of being a contentious issue, it can be helpful to set a time limit up front. Tell the reporter that you have another commitment at a given time and when that time comes, you can decide if the interview is worth continuing.

MEDIA VISUALS

When the day of your interview arrives, there are some practical elements to consider about the way that you visually present yourself. While this may seem superficial to think about, you want to ensure that you look and sound your best and nothing gets in the way of your intended message.

One of the most challenging aspects of a television interview is what to do with your hands. Using appropriate gestures or leaving your hands open at your sides work. Placing your hands in a "fig leaf" position, in your pockets, or folded is awkward and can read as defensive.

In the interest of focusing on the messages, dress as simply as possible. Pay attention to what reporters wear—many times it is one bold color, or perhaps two contrasting colors. Avoid wild patterns in clothes.

If possible, conduct the interview while you are standing rather than sitting and if not done in the studio, the background should reflect something related to your message. If the story is about science, seeing a lab behind the interviewee is more dynamic than a principal's office and also sends the message that you are an engaged leader.

If you are in the studio and must sit, move to the middle toward the edge of the seat and lean slightly forward toward the interviewer. This displays interest and engagement in the topic.

As you are responding to questions, don't forget this is a two-way conversation. Relax and focus on your breathing rate to slow down. Be friendly and warm, using the interviewer's name when you're responding to a question and answering with reference to the question so that it can't be taken out of context.

For example, if the question is, "Can you tell us more about why the plan changed?" Your answer shouldn't be, "Because we didn't receive the permit for a larger event." To provide a complete answer and stay on a positive note, say, "In an effort to work with city planners, we adjusted the size of the event while still including the fun events originally planned."

AFTER THE STORY

After the story runs, don't forget to follow up with the reporter. Thank them when they did a good job, or at least a fair job. In the event of negative press, sometimes the best you can hope for is a story that provides more context. If you believe they got it wrong, tell them and provide them with corrected information but don't overreact.

If you can remain professional in your conversation, you may be able to improve the situation. In most cases, they will not return to that story to get it right, but it may help in future stories on your school or district. That reporter will likely want to do what they can to make it right.

Keep nurturing the relationship with the reporter no matter how the initial story went. Read or watch their work and send them a note from time to time if there is a potential story that might be relevant to their audience.

TRACKING AND REPORTING

While media coverage of something is very exciting, it is important to keep it in perspective. It is a tool among many that are available to use to communicate. Choosing whether or not to put the effort into effective media outreach should be based on the objective in mind.

Are you trying to increase awareness, attendance, volunteers, or partners? Are you trying to promote a program, school, or event? Is it about educating the public about your organization's services, challenges, or opportunities? Which audiences are you trying to increase awareness with or educate?

Taking into consideration who will be reached by the outlet, is it likely that your effort with the media will be worth the effort? Are there other ways to reach that audience that require less effort or are less dependent on the reporter or other competing news?

For example, if your objective is to promote the award-winning arts program at your high school to increase enrollment there, why not put your effort into channels that allow you to specifically target middle grade students and families with an interest in art? A Facebook promotion would allow that type of specificity as well as student presentations at the schools that feed into the high school. Knowing the objective and using the right tool cuts down on time and resources spent and usually results in a better return.

ASK & ANSWER

- Do you know any of the people who work in the media in your region?
- How have you felt about media coverage of your school?
- What tips from this chapter might help you be more proactive in reaching out when you have a newsworthy story?

TWELVE

Internal Communication

The return to school for hybrid learning presented a number of challenges for schools across the nation. Plans for the reopening were rife with new COVID-19 safety protocols for staff—from temperature checks and handwashing to social distancing. For high school principal Mike Jaffe, instituting these new procedures at the district's largest high school made the task even more daunting.

District Office administration recommended that all employees utilize their school's main entrance each day to allow Main Office clerks to monitor temperature checks. The District's human resources manager's email sent to principals before the reopening provided a general outline of the new daily attendance plan with links to the Centers for Disease Control (CDC) site for recommendations. To share the information quickly, Principal Jaffe copied and pasted the section from the human resources' email into the weekly update to his staff.

Nearly one week after the high school's reopening, Principal Jaffe was besieged with staff complaints. Teachers were angry that the new procedure no longer allowed them to come in early for classroom prep because of the difference in start times for Main Office clerks. Food service staff members expressed frustration at having to now walk to the front of the building each morning after parking in the back of the building near the kitchen entrance. Security officers reported their confusion at not knowing which entrances should be opened during the day.

Overall, Principal Jaffe understood that his email to staff had done the opposite of what he intended. Rather than empower his staff with information, he had insulted, frustrated, and confused them. He recognized that his email fell short because it neglected to consider how the new protocol would impact each employee group. The needs of teachers were not the same as those of food service staff.

He realized that his email had taken a "one size fits all" approach to communicating, damaging his staff's morale. It had come across as tone-deaf and out of touch. He knew he needed to do something fast to stop the bleeding! His first plan of action was to schedule a series of meetings with leaders from each employ-ee group to listen to their concerns.

After analyzing the information collected from the meetings, he met with his administrative team to create workarounds for each group's challenges. He then assigned each member of his team to act as a liaison between his office and the various groups to troubleshoot problems, answer questions, and most important-ly, ensure future updates were shared with the specific group leaders first. Final-ly, he addressed the issue in his next staff email. He accepted responsibility for the mishap, demonstrated his understanding of their concerns, and shared his new plans to mitigate their challenges.

Weeks later, staff questions and concerns related to the new protocol had significantly decreased. Members of his administrative team reported their obser-vations that staff members were appreciative of the open line of communication Principal Jaffe had created. They felt empowered and valued by the employee-centered communication that included their feedback and respected their roles.

THE BENEFITS

When leaders think about strong internal communication, they may ima-gine the apparent benefits, fulfilled employees who enjoy coming to cam-pus. However, the investment in great internal communication goes far beyond the employee ranks. It not only strengthens the internal workings of an organization but also impacts external perceptions.

Employees are the expert on your school in their circles of influence. At their church, on the sidelines of their child's team, or at the neighbor-hood barbeque, the cafeteria worker or third grade teacher is the person folks turn to for information about the campus. If they are informed about the latest programs and excited about where they work, that is a powerful testimonial.

While many think about effective communications in terms of what is being sent out to families and community members, starting with em-ployees can reap the rewards externally by projecting a positive image, garnering community support, or helping to pass funding initiatives.

FOUR-STEP PROCESS

It can be tempting to want to throw a party or put together gifts to help lift morale, and those are not necessarily bad ideas, but without research, we don't know what will have the most powerful impact. Like any com-munication effort, internal communications should be undertaken through the four-step public relations process: research, planning, imple-mentation, and evaluation.

A survey of employees can inform us of a variety of issues. Use rating questions to ask about morale and whether they are receiving enough recognition, whether they feel their work is valued. Don't forget to also find out where they currently receive information about the school and how effective they believe those methods have been. Adding open-ended questions can be helpful for getting new ideas about how to reward employees and any new communication methods employees recommend.

On the qualitative side of research, it can be a great idea to have a one-time focus group or ongoing communications committee that is representative of employees. It can be helpful to have a group review the quantitative results of the survey and provide longer explanations of the data. In addition, a group like this can assist throughout the year in previewing communication ideas and bringing concerns to light so they can be addressed more quickly.

After an analysis of the research results, a plan can be developed. Do employees report needing more recognition? Are they receiving enough information about the vision or programs at the school? Do they have additional ideas about events or communication platforms? Using their input as a foundation, internal communication objectives and strategies can be added to a school-wide communication plan or developed as a unique plan.

The plan should include a measurable goal—What will change as a result of the internal communication efforts? Will more employees attend an event, open emails, or post positively about their work? Is it possible to conduct the same survey to measure the difference in responses?

After giving the plan a reasonable time period to have an impact, for example, six months to a year, evaluate how effective it has been against the goals that were set. If using the same survey to determine the differences, pay special attention to the open-ended questions. How did employees feel about the campaign? Did they notice the extra effort? Did they have suggestions for improvement? Even when a goal isn't met, there is always something that can be learned about the effort.

BASIC RULES

While special events and recognition programs can make employees feel valued for a certain period of time, there are some basic internal communication principles that when followed can help to ensure a positive employee climate.

- *Don't leapfrog*: If there is an exciting new program or change coming to the campus, employees should be the first to know. It doesn't feel good to hear news about your workplace from other people. Make sure that when there is news to be shared, it flows from the inside out.

- *Stay above the fray*: Over the years and budget changes, leaders are likely to encounter union versus district leadership tensions. While you might feel drawn toward one side or the other, it is important to try to stay neutral. The short-term conflicts are eventually resolved, and effective leaders reach the other side maintaining positive relationships with everyone involved.
- *Be consistent*: Ongoing communication using consistent methods of communication creates a sense of stability, especially in times of great change. Even when there is not a lot new to say, it is important to stay in contact with staff on a regular basis.
- *Use multiple methods*: Putting a message out in one way, for example, email may be great for a majority of the staff, but may still be missed or read later than it is helpful. Using a variety of communication methods for the same message doesn't take a lot of extra time and will increase the effectiveness of the outreach effort. There is a lot competing for our attention, so if an employee sees the message more than once, they are more likely to engage with it and remember it.
- *Use systems to help*: While it might sound overwhelming to send messaging out in more than one way, once your communication methods are set up, it is a small task to copy and paste the communication into a printed sheet post in the employee room or a flyer to include in mailboxes.
- *Follow the data*: As time goes on, the communication preferences of employees often change. Continuing to ask for input about methods and checking on the climate and morale helps a leader stay connected to employee's needs and evolve to meet them.
- *Check your bias*: Be aware that each of us have biases based on our backgrounds and experiences. Be humble and curious about what you don't yet know.
- *Be creative*: Take risks and use your creativity. Even when it doesn't come across perfectly, it models vulnerability.

PRAISE

While most schools have an annual employee of the month or year program, one way to take it up a notch is with spontaneous rewards targeted at specific staff behaviors. For example, if you have an instructor that is going above and beyond in learning and integrating new technology in the classroom, reward them with public praise at a schoolwide assembly and/or provide them with monetary appreciation.

Some schools even take it a step further by creating a campus innovative teacher award program and provide the winning teacher with grant funds that they can use in their classroom. No funding for something like that? That's where strong neighborhood partnerships come in—$25 in office supplies from the local store can be very rewarding.

The most important aspect is that as a leader, you are noticing and recognizing behavior that demonstrates your campus values. Then the praise becomes a reinforcement of the vision you are creating and another way of sending a message about who you are as a school.

CELEBRATE

Creating and celebrating milestones in an organization is a fantastic way to motivate and inspire. Sometimes the everyday work at a campus can be incredibly tough; milestones remind us to pay attention to the larger picture.

In the book *The Power of Moments* by Chip and Dan Heath, they describe how the John Deere company welcomes a new person to the organization. On their first day, there is a banner hanging over their desk, the background on their computer monitor has a welcome message, and their first email is from the CEO with a personalized video welcome. There is a gift on the desk—a miniature tractor, and their first lunch is planned with their immediate workgroup.

While John Deere may be a wealthy company, none of these things cost a great deal—what it took to make a new employee feel special was time and a system of doing this for every new person.

While districts may not welcome a lot of new employees, there are still a wide variety of moments to celebrate. For example, when a teacher moved from school to school or from one grade to another or a classified employee receives a promotion.

Even when there are no significant changes, there are still opportunities to reflect. For example, many classrooms celebrate the 100th day for the students, but how many days has the campus been serving families? Throw a party for the 1,000th or 30,000th day.

There are important milestones taking place all over campus each day. The number of books checked out and read, meals prepared, bus miles driven, classrooms cleaned are important achievements that contribute to the success of the school.

Endings should also be marked as important transitions. When there is a transition to something new, there is a tendency to move on quickly and focus on the next thing. However, many times there are a lot of feelings invested in projects, programs, curriculum, and campuses. It is important to pay tribute and honor the way that things in the past have served us, even if we are moving on to something new.

CONNECT

Whether formal or informal, find ways to connect to staff and connect them to each other. Mentoring the next generation of administrators at your school can be a powerful way to ensure that the positive climate you have built is carried forward. Setting up a monthly "aspiring administrators" meeting where you share an element of leadership is one way to do that. Leaving the membership open-ended rather than by invite-only ensures that everyone feels welcome and might even bring out the leadership qualities of someone you might not have thought of in that way before.

Informal mentoring like checking in with staff who seem to be a little off or having a challenging day is just as important. And mentoring doesn't need to be only one way. Finding a reverse mentor can help you as a leader stay connected to the views and perspectives of the younger people at your site, as well as help you with some of the digital skills that your staff may take for granted.

Beyond the boosting relationships between you and staff, mentoring and reverse mentoring can be incredibly beneficial among staff themselves. With a mix of veteran teachers, newer teachers, technology lovers and those who struggle with it, mixed partnerships could help teachers with all backgrounds to learn from each other. Providing valuable preparatory time to allow those relationships to blossom is a wise investment in campus connection.

Another way to motivate employees is to encourage their passions. If you have a staff member who is wild about gardening, find a way to allow them to apply that interest around the campus. No money for a stipend? Taking over their class once or twice a month will give them that valuable time.

Another way to get to know other staff and their interests is to invite staff to provide a brief presentation on a topic of their choice at staff meetings. The topic could be related to a personal passion, or perhaps about a new interactive activity they are doing that is working out well in their classroom.

In addition to connecting staff to you and each other, connect them to the campus vision and values. Every task that is happening on campus, from the cleaning of the staff bathroom to the coaching of the academic decathlon team, is connected to teaching and learning. Staying on top of ordering painting or robotic supplies is connected to teaching and learning. Preparing healthy meals and making sure kids have a donated warm jacket is connected to teaching and learning. Make it a habit to verbalize the values of the school and connect them to the work. Be explicit about those connections—agenda items in a meeting should be related to a value, office procedures should be connected to values, playground rules should be connected to values.

Lastly, to connect with staff, don't be afraid to be silly. Allow students and staff to throw pies in your face if they meet a reading goal. Agree to lip-synch a popular song or cut your hair if test scores rise to a certain number. Whatever it is that will motivate students and staff toward a goal, don't be afraid to take it on. When you are vulnerable enough to make fun of yourself and not take yourself so seriously, you give the entire staff permission to be their imperfect selves.

LISTENING

One of the biggest challenges a leader might face when it comes to making sure they are listening to staff is taking the time to do just that. There are a number of proactive suggestions in this book to help with communication, but in the case of increasing listening, sometimes the best thing that can happen is very simple—creating the time and space for an exchange of information.

In the office, this might mean that unless you are on a deadline with a project that requires some quiet concentration, your office door remains open. Even if you're not involved in the conversations, you'll hear the latest about the successes, challenges, and complaints on campus. In addition, the open door might provide the access needed for a staff member walking by to stop by and share a problem or ask for advice.

When staff does stop by, be present. Try to set aside the forms that need to be filled out, the substitutes that need to be called in or the schedule that needs to be set up. People can feel it when a leader is truly listening and sometimes they just need to be heard. Make sure that support staff know they are also welcome to stop by; many times they will be too intimidated or will want to avoid infringing on your time.

One big "aha" that came to a new principal recently was the need to filter and organize information for her staff that was coming from the district office. "There was this superhighway of information that was overwhelming and took a great deal of time to sift through," explains Phoebe A. Hearst Elementary School Principal Michelle Pechette. "It was my role to be an ambassador for vertical alignment with district initiatives and also fully support the diverse needs of my staff." Multiple methods of disseminating communication became key for her school.

One important method was to trickle the directives and initiative information to her staff in the form of scheduled weekly emails that came to them one day a week—Sundays. That way, they could have the information first thing on Monday mornings when they got back to the classroom. Staff began to anticipate the message.

Next, she would have discussions surrounding the directives in bimonthly staff meetings. These staff meeting discussions would serve as feedback loops. All of that information then went into an organized Google Doc so that teachers had a one-click access to everything they needed to meet expectations.

Along the same lines, make sure that you are valuing the time of your staff. If there is nothing on the agenda for that week's staff meeting, there is no reason to meet. If you are meeting, there should be an agenda and by the end of the meeting, a list of decisions and next steps so that the time spent in the meeting is effectively utilized. Anything that can be handled with an email or electronic poll should be.

In addition to listening to staff, listen to data and facts, especially when they are hard to hear. If you all have been working on closing the achievement gap on your campus but the data is going in the opposite direction, don't be afraid to confront it. Even if you don't know what the solution may be, it is important to be vulnerable enough to look at where the school is not living up to its promise.

That kind of vulnerability shows commitment to honesty and demonstrates character. Your staff may struggle with you to try to figure out what else can be done to better serve students in need, but they will know that you all are in the struggle together.

ASK & ANSWER

- Does your internal communication with staff represent the culture, values, and climate of your school?
- How do you determine if or when communication is best shared in person instead of by email?
- How much does staff input impact your messaging?

THIRTEEN

Culture Building

Mrs. Adalgo's sixth period history class had recently concluded a section on Christopher Columbus. Over the course of study students engaged in extensive research and dialogue about the explorer and the growing national debate surrounding the renaming of the holiday to Indigenous Peoples Day. Some students challenged the legitimacy of the Columbus "discovery" of America, while others questioned whether or not changing the name of the holiday was even meaningful.

Delighted by her student's active interest in the subject, Mrs. Adalgo sent a letter to parents encouraging them to continue the conversation at home. The following week, Principal Allen Montgomery visited Mrs. Adalgo to inquire about the letter. Over the weekend, he had received several angry emails from parents expressing their disagreement with the subject matter and the appropriateness of the discussion.

As a culturally responsive leader, Principal Montgomery knew that this moment required him to understand all the "angles" without defaulting to quick judgment. Mrs. Adalgo was a third-year teacher whose students admired and respected her for her teaching style, honesty, and ability to connect history to their current realities. In service to his year-long effort to create a culture of error at the high school, Principal Montgomery saw the issue as an opportunity rather than a problem.

His outlook was mirrored in his language and approach to Mrs. Adalgo as he shared with her some of the responses he had received from parents of her students. He then thanked her for the great teaching that not only made the lesson real for students but also generated excitement around the learning. Mrs. Adalgo was immediately put at ease by his calm, upbeat demeanor.

Principal Montgomery asked her to help him think about ways in which they could use the subject matter to educate parents. How could they show respect for the diversity of opinions without sacrificing student engagement? What addi-

109

tional communication could they have shared beforehand with parents about the history lesson to set the stage for the discussion?

By adopting a positive and collaborative posture, Principal Montgomery aided Mrs. Adalgo in being able to view the situation from a strength-based perspective rather than deficit-based. He had affirmed her teaching skill even as he encouraged her deeper analysis and critical thinking to arrive at a creative solution.

Encouraged by their conversation, Mrs. Adalgo continued the cycle and met with her colleagues in the history department to further brainstorm possible solutions. The result was the creation of a department-wide set of guidelines for parents titled, How to Talk to Your Child About History. Principal Montgomery's focused effort to create a school culture that rewarded innovation and allowed for mistakes had produced a team of educators unafraid to think critically and work collaboratively.

Left without any intervention, each school will develop a culture, but it won't necessarily serve students, staff, and the community very well. A healthy culture is created; it does not organically develop without intentional focus.

Like a garden, building culture demands consistency and the necessary ingredients for success. In a garden, that would include seeds, soil, water, sun, and nutrients. In the case of school culture, those ingredients include trust, accountability, purpose, and connection.

In the book *Teach Like a Champion 2.0* by Doug Lemov, the author describes a "culture of error," an environment where educators feel like they can make mistakes and collaboration is encouraged to develop creative solutions. In a culture where educators are taking risks, they will sometimes fail, but they will also discover new and better ways to serve students and families.

According to Lemov, the culture of error fosters more critical thinking, creativity, collaboration, and a focus on deeper analysis. Developing this type of culture is about trust and connection. From a communications perspective, it means using language that demonstrates it is "safe to be wrong." For example, rather than talking about problems, frame them as opportunities. Rather than talking about blame, refocus on what is learned, what needs to be explored and future solutions. This is very similar to the "growth mindset" approach many schools use with students.

Vulnerability is at the heart of developing this type of staff engagement. Although it is sometimes treated as a weakness, vulnerability demonstrates a leader's "human" side. When a leader is authentic enough to admit their own mistakes and frailties, they give everyone around them permission to do the same.

When a teacher is promoted to an administrative position, they may feel like they need to demonstrate their knowledge and competence to their new team. However, admitting you don't know everything and truly listening and learning from the teachers and support staff on campus can increase trust tremendously. When the team feels respected, they will be far more likely to admit when they are struggling and ask for help.

CLEAR EXPECTATIONS

One of the most important steps a leader can make is to develop clear expectations that are consistent with the stated values of the school and district. If the school has signage around campus saying that they value diversity, friendship, and kindness—is that meant for just the students? How are those values reflected and modeled in the way that the adults on campus treat each other?

Bring the school community together, including family representatives and support staff, to operationalize those values. Define the core of what those words mean and develop a list of sample behaviors you might expect to see under each one. Everyone likes to feel a part of something bigger. Encourage everyone connected to the campus to ask this fundamental question: "What is your contribution to students and learning?"

Connect the actions that the school is taking to these core values in an explicit way. For example, if you are bringing in a Portuguese folk dancing group for a performance, make sure in your newsletter, website, and social media posts that you are referring back to diversity as a core value and why it is important to learning and growing.

Drill down into all the positions at the school with the people that serve in these roles—how is each person connected to these values? How can they do the job in ways that are directly tied to the values? Document these expectations so that job interviews contain value-based questions and new employees are clear about the role.

Making more connections explicit can be very helpful for staff, keeping them motivated and supportive of the shared vision. If a difficult decision is being made, it is natural to feel defensive about it and shut down discussion—but it is the worst thing a leader can do. The key to showing employees you are consistent and fair is communication. Be transparent about how difficult something is, all the factors, and the input that is considered. The more a school community understands about why a decision was made, the more likely they are to assume good intentions and defend the school leadership in discussions. People may not agree with the final decision, but if they believe that both sides were heard and a fair decision was made, most will eventually come around.

An important element of this process is to set the expectation for open and intense debate while an issue is being decided, but unification around the decision once it happens. It is also important to circle back around on particularly difficult topics and ensure that everyone on the team is on the same page moving forward.

Few things are more stressful than not knowing what is expected. Our collective experiences with COVID-19 have demonstrated that distrust breeds in an uncertain environment. There will of course be experiences a school leader will face that are unpredictable with solutions that evolve over time. Ongoing and transparent communication is the antidote to fear and uncertainty. The more fear-inducing the situation, the more often the community involved needs to hear from a leader, even if what they hear is that nothing has changed since the last message.

As Patrick Lencioni describes in his book *Five Dysfunctions of a Team*, trust is the foundation of an effective team. Woven into the story of a fictional technology company with a new leader, the book explores how absence of trust negatively impacts teams, leading to fear of conflict, lack of commitment, avoidance of accountability, and inattention to results.

BUILDING TRUST

After involving a variety of people in creating a shared vision and collective values, a number of communication tools can build on that foundation. One of the most important rules is to avoid "jumping over" internal audiences. Nothing demonstrates respect more than trusting your employees with important information, particularly when it is negative and potentially damaging. Trust can erode quickly when a team member learns about something negative about their employer from the media or other outside source.

Empower the members of your team through communication. Think of it as a function that is woven into every decision and makes communicating an expectation. In a staff meeting, the last question should be to ask how the information will be communicated. For complicated issues, make sure your staff have access to discussion points. Remember that in their spheres of influence, they are the experts on your school. Make sure they have the facts and details available to promote your program and debunk rumors.

Provide some time at an all-campus meeting to develop school elevator speeches where employees can work on what they might say about your campus strengths if someone they know asks about where they work and how they like it.

If a difficult issue is developing or a new program is about to launch, preview it with staff. Hold a brown bag lunch talk where they can bring their meal, get information about the issue or program, and ask questions or provide ideas about how to deal with certain aspects they are most familiar with. For example, the school attendance clerk may be able to point out a challenge in how to access information in a new Student Information System because it is something they use every day.

Include staff as often as possible in decision-making with formal and informal opportunities for input. Engaged employees have ideas that may be helpful now or down the road. When leaders disregard their ideas without consideration, they disengage from the common purpose and instead begin to treat the school as just a job.

Help employees feel comfortable proposing new ways to get things done by asking them about what is most challenging, what takes up a lot of their time, where they see room for improvement. You might not always be able to use their ideas at that moment, but communicate why you didn't go forward with it and try to come up with a different approach to meet the underlying need.

Make sure that you are not just listening to those who are easy to listen to—namely those who are already in your corner or on the same page. With most issues, there are a variety of perspectives to consider—how have you reached out to hear the teacher voices, the support staff voices, the family voices, and the student voices? For example, if you're thinking about a menu change in the cafeteria, how about a taste test focus group with a variety of students to get their feedback?

Most importantly, seek out critics for input. They will weigh in on issues eventually, and it is almost always better if the negative or critical feedback is heard earlier. There may be a valid concern that can be addressed before a program has been pushed out to all classrooms. Remember the tip from chapter 13 on customer service—even complaints are just information. The squeaky wheel in a staff meeting may be in the minority and afraid to speak up. Anonymous surveys can be very helpful in getting valuable feedback from those who are not as vocal but have great ideas when getting their voices heard anonymously.

THE LITTLE THINGS

While planning the big things and communicating the big ideas, don't forget to do the small things that help people continue to feel personally connected to their leadership. Every employee wants to work for more than a paycheck. They want to know that the people steering the ship care about them and that what they do matters.

People thrive when they work for those they respect and admire—and with and for people who respect and admire them. Connection is personal, so take the time to see and appreciate the person, not just the worker. A kind word in a meeting, a quick discussion about family while in the hallway, an informal conversation in a doorway to ask if an employee needs help can all go a long way.

Remember their family member names, their favorite sports team, their favorite snack. Bring it to the office every once in a while to let them know you thought of them. Commiserate when their team loses the big game and cheer with them when they win.

While most communication has gone digital, it makes old-fashioned notes and cards even more valuable. Send a note after a teacher does a good job emceeing the spelling bee. Send a card after you hear about the loss of the maintenance guy's mother. Those gestures on good days and bad can be a powerful reminder that the place they work is more than their employer.

Get in the habit of celebrating people and it will become the culture. Open each meeting with an opportunity for staff to give a shout out to someone on campus who deserves the attention. Make sure you are evening out the praise by recognizing the employees who are less popular. It's easy to recognize your best employees because they're consistently doing awesome things. However, is it possible that maybe consistent recognition is a reason they're your best employees?

Every employee, even a relatively poor performer, does something well. You might have to work hard to find reasons but a few words of recognition, especially in public, may be the nudge an average performer needs to up their game.

Even out the critical feedback as well. No employee is perfect. Everyone needs constructive guidance, even if it is small ways to improve their skill set. For example, great bosses provide criticism in private and praise in public, so make sure you are not unintentionally shaming a team member by forgetting who else is in earshot.

The words of guidance matter as well. The culture of error, Lemov argues, shifts staff (and students) away from a "deficit perspective" to a "strength perspective." That means framing feedback with what is possible rather than what is missing.

HIRING FOR CULTURE

One of the easiest ways to impact the culture is to hire people who make it positive. Obviously, it is much more difficult to work with a challenging staff member, guiding them to change their mindset over time. Hiring people who show up on day one with a passion for the job and the purpose is ideal. However, people who are in charge of hiring have to also ensure that their personal implicit bias doesn't color hiring results.

It is natural for people to be drawn to other people like them and believe that those individuals would be a great team "fit." Unfortunately, sometimes that instinctual pull can blind us to people that can bring something even more important—diversity of thought that ultimately changes the culture and makes our organization even stronger.

One way to ensure that implicit bias is neutralized to the degree possible is to integrate important culturally responsive questions in job applications and interviews. This will help set the right expectations for potential employees and allow hiring panels to see strengths from a deeper and more diverse perspective. For example, what is the person's cultural awareness regarding race, ability, sexual orientation, gender identity, and other social identities? How would they describe their ability to communicate and collaborate with people across lines of difference with respect and dignity? How might they provide culturally sensitive care to promote the reduction of systemic barriers?

These questions might not seem like an important aspect of being a librarian, for example. But someone who has a culturally responsive mindset will approach the work in a completely different way. They might apply a lens of equity, for example, to the books that are selected for students, ensuring that there are a wide variety of books written by authors of color. They might also hang artwork that highlight the achievements of people with diverse backgrounds and provide programming that challenges and engages students to read selections outside their normal comfort zone.

ASK & ANSWER

- How would you describe the culture of your campus?
- Do you believe your campus is a safe place to risk and make mistakes?
- In what ways can you contribute to a healthier campus culture?

FOURTEEN

Customer Service

The weeks leading up to the senior prom at Union Senior High School were always the busiest for frontline office staff. Each day saw a barrage of phone calls from parents with questions about everything from prom fees to form deadlines. Front office receptionist Mrs. Jones, doing her best to answer questions, soon became overwhelmed with fielding phone calls even as she sought to serve the throng of parents standing in front of her.

While she had enough information to respond quickly to some parent inquiries, there were times when she would need to place callers on hold to go and find answers to their questions. Naturally, after several days, this method created a bottleneck of long lines and wait times as parents became increasingly agitated. As a result, Mrs. Jones' demeanor soon gave way to frustration resulting in a terse and defensive tone when fielding phone calls and face-to-face inquiries.

Principal Lisa Maxwell's office was flooded with emails and calls from parents complaining that the school receptionist was unfit for the job. "Why doesn't she know anything?" some emailed. Others protested, "How long do I have to wait for an answer to my question?!" Despite Mrs. Jones' tenure as the longest serving secretary in the front office, Principal Maxwell decided a meeting was necessary to better understand the issue.

Fifteen minutes into their conversation Principal Maxwell understood why and how Mrs. Jones was challenged to provide good customer service to parents. She explained nearly 70 percent of the calls from parents regarding prom happened during the first hour of the school day. Responding to their inquiries precluded her from being able to efficiently handle parent visitors, deal with students entering the office, and her other morning duties.

Principal Maxwell also learned that most of the parents entering the office were there to pay their student's prom fee which required Mrs. Jones to leave the front desk temporarily to place money in the safe. As the building leader, Princi-

pal Maxwell understood the underlying frustrations of both her parents and Mrs. Jones due to a lack of training, communication, and support.

First, she directed the teacher serving as the senior prom sponsor to record a message with important dates, deadlines, and information about the prom to be added to the school's phone system. Parents would then have immediate access to information about the event without needing to be put on hold. Next, she instructed her administrative assistant to be responsible for morning fee collection and safe deposits to help reduce the number of parents waiting in line to make payments.

Lastly, she worked with Mrs. Jones to develop a script based on answers to frequently asked questions along with weekly updates from the senior class sponsor. She encouraged her to view her role as an air traffic controller charged with leading parents to find the information they needed. They then brainstormed important questions such as, "Could the answer already be posted to the high school's website?" "Was there a Senior Parent Newsletter that contained the information that they may have missed?" "Did social media provide more opportunities to share updates?"

When armed with information and additional internal support, frontline staff need not dread their role as resourceful and knowledgeable customer service agents.

CRITICISM AS INFORMATION

In today's educational environment, families have a wide variety of choices and don't necessarily take their child to the neighborhood school by default. Marketing the special programs on a campus is a great strategy, but ultimately many potential families will judge a school based on how they are treated by the office staff, leaders, support staff, and teachers. If it is a poor experience, not only will the school likely lose that student, but also the family will likely tell several others about it.

On the other hand, a great experience can greatly improve a school's competitiveness. When people feel connected to the staff at a campus, they are likely to stay and they are likely to tell others about how much they enjoy their school. Therefore, the smart school leader will ensure that campus personnel understand the value of customer service and set high expectations in this area.

When a parent walks through the front office door and begins shouting at the school secretary, it can be uncomfortable, jarring, and even downright scary. It would be wonderful if the feedback we need to hear about our schools always came wrapped in a calm, polite package.

Many times, however, the most important data we might receive about our system comes in the form of an angry encounter. Even if it is presented in a very harsh way, from a systemic perspective it is just information. It may be information the school or district desperately needs to know.

As Winston Churchill once said, "Criticism may not be agreeable, but it is necessary. It fulfills the same function as pain in the human body. It calls attention to an unhealthy state of things. If it is heeded in time, danger may be averted; if it is suppressed, a fatal distemper may develop."

Negative feedback can tell us a number of things—it might suggest that we need to change a program or policy, provide personnel training, or increase communication to clear up a misunderstanding. It takes a healthy organization and leadership to be vulnerable enough to recognize the need for change rather than disregard or undercut the complaint.

It is the responsibility of a school leader to listen to critical voices and champion them, even when it's difficult. Perhaps especially when it is difficult. Being courageous and listening to stakeholders means following the information provided even when it contradicts current leadership beliefs.

SETTING OFFICE STANDARDS

Developing the ability to take in complaints without defensiveness is a valuable skill that can be learned. In fact, although few employees receive formal training in the area, many of the most effective customer service skills are tools that can be learned. Even if staff received training at some point, it is a skill set that needs to be refreshed from time to time.

Public-facing staff would benefit from formal training in a number of areas. For example, what standards does the school have for how people who come into the office are greeted? Is there an immediate acknowledgment when someone walks in? Even if a staff member is busy helping another person, do they look up, make eye contact, and smile so the visitor knows they've been seen and acknowledged?

How about phone calls to the school office? Do staff pick up the phone before three rings to let someone know they will be with them soon or let it go to voicemail? What kind of voicemail message does the school have in place? The recorded message is a great opportunity to answer common questions as well as brag about recent school accomplishments.

Does the school office have consistent hours posted in a variety of ways and is there always at least one staff member available during those times? Imagine a parent taking valuable time away from their job to come to campus to turn in a form or talk with a counselor, only to find that there is no one available and they will have to wait until after a lunch break or take more time away from work to come back another time.

Being transparent about office hours and accountable to the posted hours is a matter of equity. Not every parent has the kind of employment that is generous about time away from work. Value their time and ensure that they are able to quickly and easily conduct school business when they visit.

SOLVING PROBLEMS

It may not be possible to immediately solve a caller's issue. They may have reached someone on the phone who is in another department or the person they need to speak with is out of the office. Too many times, the response is to place the burden on the caller, asking them to call another place or during another time to address the issue. The customer doesn't care "who" is responsible for "what," she only knows she needs help.

The best response is to take ownership of the issue that lands at your desk. If you can't help, find out who in the system can help and make the connection for the caller. That may include taking the information down and making sure someone gets back to the caller. If possible, stay on the call with the person while you try the other office and if you get an answer, explain the issue before you pass the caller to the next person. Employees are far more likely to be able to understand the issue and explain it using internal terminology so that it gets addressed correctly.

Empathy goes a long way with someone who is dealing with a challenge. Even if an employee believes the fault lies with the person who comes in the door, the frustration they are feeling should be acknowledged. A simple, "I'm so sorry that happened, let's work together to fix it" works far better than saying, "Well, you should have read the enrollment packet" or even worse, putting the visitor through a series of questions that make them feel embarrassed at missing something. It is a sure way to put them on the defensive and actually increase the amount of time it will take to solve the problem.

Sometimes, all a customer needs is a chance to let their frustration out. A well-trained office employee lets them vent and doesn't take it personally. Giving the person the opportunity to share their experience and challenges can take the initial tension out of the encounter and clear a path to solving the issue.

Actively listening to their story and then paraphrasing the key points makes the customer feel respected. Empathizing with their feelings about the experience is also validating and can de-escalate a situation. That doesn't mean the employee agrees with the customer's view on the issue, but that they understand the customer's experience is not up for debate.

Once the visitor or caller has had a chance to explain their experience and feels heard, both parties can move into solutions. If possible, offer compromise or ask for their input about how to solve the problem. When you make the customer your problem-solving partner, they move from a complaint mindset to a solution mindset, requiring them to be creative and come up with ideas rather than just criticize. Ask, "What do you think would be fair?" or suggest a few options by saying, "Here are a couple of things we can do" and allow them to weigh in.

It can be hard to experience the treatment of someone who is angry with the school, but it can help to re-frame that anger as care and concern. Too many students don't have someone in their life that is an advocate, so even when it comes to our door in an unpleasant package, that kind of advocacy should be welcomed. Seeing the interaction that way can also help with not taking the situation personally.

It might not be possible to solve the issue with one interaction. If that is the case, commit to a time to follow up and connect before that time, even if it is just to say that you are still working on it. You may not be the only person the customer is reaching out to, so when there is an ongoing issue, be sure to give your team a heads-up so you all are on the same page and prepared to help.

DIVERSITY

Another element to consider in providing great service are the differences in how groups engage with tasks and relationships differently. It can be easy to assume that everyone we encounter sees an interaction in the same way we do, but our cultural background greatly influences what we experience.

For example, people who were raised with more individualistic influences are more likely to be very task-oriented. In that mindset, we want to move through any introductory discussion quickly and get to the task at hand. For these individuals, timelines and rules are strict—if you say you will be somewhere at 2 p.m., you are likely there at least five minutes early.

That works well when there are two similarly minded people engaging with each other. They don't take it personally if there isn't much personal discussion and they appreciate being able to get in and out with their task completed quickly.

However, someone raised with more collectivist influences will see the engagement differently. They are more likely to want to have enough of a conversation to feel comfortable before moving on to the task. They may ask about your family and expect that you will ask about theirs. Relationships and people are of prime importance and come before rules and timelines, so 2 p.m. is a suggestion that could turn into 2:30 p.m. or even 3:00 p.m. That doesn't mean they don't care about the task, it's just that they care more about the people involved.

Paying attention to those differences can help inform practices, policies, and the way that you might approach solving a problem. With one group you might point to the written policy in the student handbook. For another, you may want to use a collectivist approach and appeal to how the rule makes the campus a safer place for all.

WORD CHOICES

In addition to approaching the interaction with the right mindset and understanding different perspectives, there are some specific phrases that can greatly impact the success of the encounter. Some examples of phrases to avoid include:

- *"That's not my job"*—when you are the person that a customer connects with, you represent the school. Even if what they are asking is not something you can take care of, there is still a way to help them find someone who can.
- *"No one can help you right now"*—as an employee, if you are available then someone can help, even if that help is to take the information and follow up.
- *"It wasn't my/our fault"*—discussion of fault rarely leads to a productive place, listen and move to solutions.
- *"Sorry, our policy on that is . . ."*—Make sure your policies serve students and families and take the time to explain them. If they are no longer serving all families well, it may be time to review them.

On the other side of the coin, there are some positive phrases that can improve the climate:

- *Their name*—learn and refer to your customer by name when you can, it gives the conversation a personal touch.
- *"Thank you for calling/returning my call"*—show your customer you feel their call and time is important.
- *"How may I help you?"*—open the lines of communication on a positive note by giving your customer an offer of assistance.
- *Being offered a choice to be placed on hold or called back*—ask permission to place them on hold so they can decide if they would rather call back later.
- *"I'm sorry to keep you waiting/Thank you for waiting"*—no one likes to be kept waiting, but a simple apology or acknowledgment can keep the customer from feeling resentment.
- *"Thank you for calling this to our attention"*—encouraging feedback from your customer is the best way to continue good service and ensure satisfaction.
- *"What else can I do for you today?"*—This is a good way to end your conversation with your customer and to be sure their needs were met.

OTHER CUSTOMER SERVICE OPPORTUNITIES

The bus is the first contact for many students and families and can set the tone for their day. Greeting students with a smile is a great start. Getting to know riders, using their first name, and learning about the special events in their lives creates a wonderful bond. When a bus driver is connecting with students at a deeper level, they will be able to identify when they are having a rough day, try to help, and even notify the school to look out for the student.

In the cafeteria, greet students as they are picking up trays and try to find a reason to compliment them. Create an inviting environment through what is displayed, how the room is decorated and how the food is presented. Think of the cafeteria more like inviting someone to your home to eat. When possible, try to connect lunchtimes with classroom lessons. Ask teachers to provide ideas that tie in with what they are doing at the same time. For example, food from different cultures or countries, pieces of an apple to teach fractions, or calorie counts and comparisons to amount of exercise needed for math or health class.

Around the outside of the school, try to view your campus as a visitor. Are there areas that need to be cleaned up? Is it easy to find the office and park near it? Is the signage helpful and welcoming? Is it provided in the variety of languages that are used at your school?

How are the adults on campus interacting with students? Are there positive interactions in the hallway? Are employees easy to identify though a badge or clothing?

Is there evidence of joy? Is there a display case of positive things related to students and staff? Is there a calendar of school and community events? Is there a suggestion box or information about how to get more involved with the school?

All of these questions can help guide a school leader to demonstrate pride in the campus which is infectious and spreads quickly to staff and students, as well as being evident to visitors and potential students.

ASK THEM

Another idea to use data to increase transparency is a customer service survey of families *and* school site employees to rate the service levels of district office departments. This is an extremely vulnerable and coura-geous step to take and hopefully reflects a sincere interest in improving service to families and schools. One of the surprising outcomes in some of these surveys is the difference in how departments are perceived by families versus school staff. When the results come back, any customer service training can incorporate specific weak areas and provide exam-ples that hit the mark.

ASK & ANSWER

- What mechanism do you have in place for frontline staff to share their issues or concerns with you?
- Is your frontline staff provided with scripts to answer important questions regarding new initiatives or during a crisis?
- Have you trained your frontline staff on conflict resolution or de-escalation techniques?

Supplemental training materials available for this chapter at www.schoolprpro.com/the-communicating-principal.

Part IV

Evaluating

FIFTEEN

Measuring Your Work

Sean Russell was excited to begin his tenure as principal at his alma mater McKinley High School. He had fond memories and developed lasting friendships with students of all races, ethnicities, and socioeconomic backgrounds.

However, the once highly regarded high school was losing teachers, seeing a decline in enrollment, and facing concerns that the curriculum had become less rigorous. Even more disturbing for Principal Russell was his review of students taking AP courses where he noticed students of color were woefully underrepresented. Advanced placement courses not only expose students to a more rigorous curriculum but also are a strong factor in college admissions.

He knew that something had to be done and set a goal to increase sign-up for advanced placement courses for students of color. A meeting with his administrative team helped him understand the historical background and provided context for his analysis of data. However, the question he had yet to answer was, "Why were African American and Latinx students not signing up?"

Principal Russell began by creating a series of surveys for his teachers and families of color. He asked questions related to attitudes and perceptions about college-level courses, barriers to signing up for the classes, and expectations for student achievement. Existing national data suggested that among African American and Latinx students with a high degree of readiness for AP, only about half were participating.

Analysis of the responses showed the need for a cultural shift among teaching staff concerned about the students' "readiness" for advanced courses. The survey revealed high anxiety for the families of students of color, who worried about the potential for failure and the costs related to the exam.

Next, Principal Russell set a timeline for the first semester to engage parents and students of color in an awareness campaign focused on sharing the benefits of AP Courses. He worked with guidance counselors to host an AP Fair, where students could speak directly to their peers about the classes, and a Parent

University for parents to speak to AP teachers and ask questions. Lastly, he coordinated a series of Lunch N' Learns for teachers to explore the impact of their belief systems, approaches, and expectations for successful recruitment and retention of students of color.

Over the next semester, Principal Russell continued to monitor the results of his communication campaign. He issued another survey to the same target groups gauging their awareness of AP Courses at McKinley High. Noting the significant increase in the percentage of families stating their awareness of the AP Program, he was confident his objective had been met. Most importantly, understanding the needs, challenges, and aspirations of this stakeholder group would allow him greater insight when tracking AP enrollment numbers among Black and Latinx students in the future.

Even when people are determined to follow the four-step process, conduct foundational research, track their efforts, and evaluate their success, there seems to be a stumbling block when it comes to developing truly measurable objectives for a communications campaign. Perhaps it is the fear that they won't meet the objective that drives the reluctance to document the hoped-for outcome. Developing a culture that accepts that objectives won't always be met and that sometimes we learn more when they are not is key.

There are three main elements that make up a truly measurable objective. It must be time-bound, audience specific, and document a measurable phenomenon (action, perception, awareness, etc.). There are a couple of exceptions to the rule that will be discussed later in the chapter.

TIME-BOUND

If an objective is not made time-bound, then there is always a possibility that it could happen at some point—the effort could simply continue into infinity. You can never fail at an objective without an associated time period. To set one, think through the amount of time it will take to have the intended impact on the intended audience. Look at how long it has taken other schools or districts to do the same thing if that data is available. If that doesn't provide any guidance, you can always take a general approach with an annual measurement.

The central question that must be answered is, "When will it happen?" The answer depends on the effort and may be a month and year, an event date, or even a survey date. For example, enrollment to rise a certain amount by the state attendance audit date or for perception to go up by the annual communication and culture survey in May. There is no wrong answer to this question, it is just a matter of committing to look for change at a certain time.

AUDIENCE SPECIFIC

The first step to making your objective audience specific is to narrow it down to your key audiences. That doesn't mean your messages and strategies won't impact other audiences, it just means that as a result of conducting and analyzing the data, the audiences that will be the most helpful in the campaign are identified as "key." There are two factors to consider when narrowing to key audiences—what is the group that will be the most impacted by the issue and what is the group that is the most influential with the impacted group?

In addition to developing measurable objectives, identifying key audiences is very helpful for messaging. The more specific the message, the more likely it will speak to the intended audience—their hopes, aspirations, challenges, beliefs, and perceptions. General messages are not nearly as impactful as those designed with an audience in mind.

Key audiences might be fifth through seventh grade families if the district is working on future changes to graduation requirements and the seventh graders will be the first affected class. A key audience might also be a group unrelated to the school. For example, a campaign in the Los Angeles area discovered that a group of folk dance teachers were highly influential with mothers in the area, well regarded and respected. Even though they had no formal association with the organization, that made them a key audience to include in activities, messaging, and measuring.

One of the most important reasons to narrow to key audiences in a communication effort is to measure. If a campaign's messages and strategies are designed to impact a particular group and as a result of checking in with that specific audience through a survey or through observable behavior, that campaign is falling short, it can be adjusted. If the focus for the campaign is too broad, the strategies may not be working with the most impactful audience groups, but that failure can be hidden by the positive response of other groups.

MEASURABLE ACTION

Selecting and focusing on the action is the last step in the objective development process. There are three questions to ask in deciding on the action that will be measured. What change do you want to see, in terms of behavior, perception, knowledge, support, or something else? Secondly, how much change do you want to see? In most cases, this looks like a percentage increase or a number increase over where things are before the campaign starts. Lastly, the piece that is sometimes missing is how exactly will you measure it? If there is no way to measure something, it is impossible to include it in a measurable objective.

There are a number of behaviors (observed and self-reported) that can be included in a measurable objective. An increase in enrollment, an increase in positive perception, a decrease in truancy, or an increase in support are all examples of the typical behaviors included in a school communication plan.

The amount of change gets a little trickier. For example, it could be a 10 percent increase, fifty more participants in an event, or twenty-five new students in a school. It is hard to know how challenging one should make the objective. Looking back at trend lines in a certain area can be very helpful. If a school has been steadily losing ten students a year, perhaps a healthy objective is to shoot for stabilizing enrollment and not losing a student in the coming year. If a school or district hasn't been tracking the area that is to be measured, it can help to look at examples in other similar-sized districts. Typically, the National School Public Relations Association (NSPRA) or a state-sponsored chapter of NSPRA can help with identifying other schools and districts that have conducted similar campaigns.

How to measure the change is the last part of the behavior piece. Measurements can include self-reported information about awareness, perception, and support gathered in pre-campaign and post-campaign surveys about the behavior; attendance tracking at events; enrollment tracking at schools; or even a vote tally in an election.

It can be tempting to include social media analytics in this area. If the objective is to gain followers so that they have access to information that supports student learning, a case can be made to use an increase in followers as a measurable objective. However, unless the measurable behavior is tied to action that supports student learning, it may simply be an output, or tool used to keep the campaign on track.

Measurable objectives are incredibly useful not only for measuring a campaign's success but also for providing clarity and focus during the campaign. In the course of developing and implementing a communication campaign, it is part of the process to come up with a wide variety of strategies and tactics and only a subset of the ideas created may be viable due to the budget, staffing, or time available. Clearly defined measurable objectives provide a helpful filter. Which strategies and tactics are likely to meet the objective? While all of the strategies may be interesting, some of them will better meet the objective. Table 15.1 provides the main questions to consider in developing a truly measurable objective and measurement ideas related to each.

EXCEPTIONS TO THE RULE

There will be times when it seems impossible to create a truly measurable objective for a campaign. One of the most frequent reasons is that the

Table 15.1.

Objective Question	Examples
Who do you hope to impact with your efforts?	Students, families, teachers, staff, community members
What change do you want to see—behavior, perception, knowledge, support?	Increased enrollment, increase in positive perception, decrease in truancy, increase in support
How much change do you want to see?	10% increase or decrease, 50 more participants, 25 new students
How exactly will you measure it?	Pre/post surveys, enrollment audit day, attendance data
By when will it happen?	Month and year, event date, survey date

school or district has never measured that behavior before, so it is impossible to set a percent or whole number increase or decrease. If that is the case, the objective could be to create a baseline for measuring the behavior. For example, in a school that has never asked stakeholders about their communication preferences, the objective might be to survey this year to create a baseline rating for each communication tool and to annually survey stakeholder groups to track changes in preferences each year.

In other cases, it may be impossible to measure due to a lack of resources. For example, if the campaign is done in a hurry to achieve something time-bound and there is no time for a pre-survey or if the school is lacking the funds, expertise, or political will to accurately measure the behavior. While not ideal, sometimes campaigns will need to be measured by outputs rather than the impact on behavior. For example, if a school doesn't have the time or money to do the pre/post survey or if there have already been several surveys that year, some outputs like social media analytics, positive media coverage, or the number of emails opened could serve as viable options. Outputs are also important reflections of effort. Even if a campaign misses the mark, outputs help to tell the story of the amount of work that was involved.

WHAT HAPPENS IF WE FAIL?

If a measured objective is set correctly, it is aspirational, something to work toward. That means that there will be times that a campaign doesn't quite hit the mark. That's when the best learning happens. When a campaign is successful, there is rarely a discussion about what didn't go well. When the overall objectives are met, there is (maybe) a brief celebration and movement on to the next communication challenge or opportunity.

When a campaign doesn't hit the mark, there is a natural tendency to find out why. Whether it is professional curiosity, a desire to get better, or simply to provide an explanation to leadership, there is a much greater effort to dig into the details.

Perhaps it was the messaging, did it fall short in communicating the benefits? Maybe it was a particular tool that wasn't appropriate for a specific audience. Output measures such as open rates and clicks on links can tell an important story about both. Pulling together a debriefing group of the key audiences can also provide invaluable information as long as the questions are open-ended enough for them to explain why they think people didn't respond to the campaign in the way it was hoped.

EXAMPLES

It can be helpful to see some examples of objectives that are truly measurable as well as some that just sound that way. Let's start with the latter:

"Improve perception of ABC Middle School"—While this sounds like a worthwhile goal, it is impossible to measure this behavior. Does everyone's perception of ABC Middle School matter or are their key audiences that influence decisions around enrollment? Naming the audience is an important element of a measurable objective. What about the timeline? If there is no set time, then the objective can never be measured. How much should the perception improve? Is one person's opinion improving a worthy target for the expenditure of taxpayer funds and staff time a campaign will require?

A better way to write the objective in a way that is measurable might be, "Improve fifth and sixth grade family member perceptions of ABC Middle School by 5 percent as measured by the annual satisfaction survey in May 2018." There is a clear definition of the audience, time period, and action that will be measured.

How about this one: "Increase attendance at XYZ High School." This is trickier because it could be argued that technically there is an implied audience as students are the ones who enroll. There is also somewhat of an implied measurement of action because if even one more student enrolls at XYZ High School, the objective is met. However, there is no time limit so the campaign could continue indefinitely, hoping for that one student to enroll.

A more defined and reasonable objective would read, "Increase attendance by 20 percent at XYZ High School prior to October 2019." The audience is still implied, but the action increase and timeline are explicit. In October 2019, there will be a definitive answer about whether or not this objective was met.

School leaders are used to paying attention to data and implementing interventions to meet academic objectives in the classroom. Treating school communication efforts with the same seriousness will allow leaders to accurately track efforts and predict the messages, channels, and tactics that will help them meet outreach objectives more easily and effectively.

ASK & ANSWER

- Do you have measurable objectives for communication at your school?
- How do you know if your communication effort is successful?
- In what areas do you plan to create a baseline so that you can measure efforts?

SIXTEEN

Data Collection

Mr. Allan Northam, a first-year principal at Scott Joplin Elementary School, is a hardworking administrator who is known to run a tight ship. One of his students happens to be the child of a board member. Mr. Northam has a track record of successfully balancing serving the dual needs of school board members who are also parents. However, lately, Board Member Jensen was flooding his office with phone calls expressing concern about negative comments she read from parents on her Facebook page.

Mrs. Jensen tends to advocate for her board and policy positions via social media and encourages community members to reach out to her with their concerns. Unfortunately, her reactions to parent complaints had started to create a cycle of alarm.

A parent took to social media to express frustration that her child was not being served lunch. After her post circulated, the conversation thread grew to include questions about why the child wasn't being provided lunch, possible theories as to why it was being withheld, and eventually, outrage at the school principal for allowing it to happen.

Mr. Northam then received an angry call from Mrs. Jensen stating, "Everyone is talking about this and I can't believe that you are denying children lunch!" Mr. Northam explained that the student in question was not denied a lunch but had been repeatedly admonished by his teacher for spending most of his lunch hour socializing rather than eating. His teacher reported that when the bell rang signaling the lunch period was over, the student would toss most of his uneaten lunch in the garbage.

Eager to find a solution to the problem, Mr. Northam quickly emailed his staff to be more flexible and allow students extra time to finish their lunches. After two weeks of following the principal's directive, teachers and lunch staff started to complain. The additional time allowed had begun to negatively impact passing schedules. Teachers' aides waited to escort stragglers back to class and lunch staff was no longer able to clean in between lunch periods.

After hearing from the teachers' union on the matter, Mr. Northam was directed by the superintendent to return to the former procedure that encouraged students to limit conversations and eat within their designated lunch period. Ultimately, Principal Northam learned an invaluable lesson about rejecting assumptions and utilizing data (e.g., observational, staff, and student survey responses) before making changes or decisions. Leaders should beware of reactionary responses that alter school systems and structures without justification and strategic communication planning.

As a school or district administrator, it may come as a surprise to find a chapter of a communications book dedicated to data. While schools are accustomed to collecting data about just about everything that happens in a classroom, when people think about communication and public relations (PR), they may think that it is a purely creative field meant for people who are more artistic. They imagine the best PR people simply have an innate and mysterious talent for knowing exactly what to say and when to say it.

There is some truth to that perspective. Most people who work in communications and PR do have a way with words, but many times what feeds that skill is a great deal of experience in which they are unintentionally storing away data about what works and doesn't work with a variety of audiences. The best in the field make that data gathering creative and explicit, searching out new information and reviewing even the most inspired ideas with potential audiences and trusted advisors. Any school leader that has an interest in improving communications at a school or campus can and should put the same data to work in their efforts.

While it may seem there is little connection between creative PR tactics and the gathering and use of data, they are two halves of the development of highly effective campaigns. Data allows us to fully understand the nature of a challenge or opportunity, demonstrates the most powerful tools to use for specific audiences, and helps us track and evaluate our efforts so that we continue to improve our practice. It is not so different from the data approach in improving student learning outcomes in classrooms. Table 16.1 provides a quick reference to the types of questions data can help answer.

Table 16.1.

Data helps us to understand the issue and plan to effectively address it	
Who are your audiences?	Most impacted
	Most influential
What do you know about them?	Preferences
	Concerns
	Demographics
How will you know if you're successful?	Feedback
	Behavior

UNDERSTANDING THE ISSUE

When a challenge or opportunity is presented to a school community, it is tempting to jump in and want to develop a quick fix, especially when someone in leadership is demanding exactly that. For example, a school board member steps into the office and announces, "We have an urgent issue! Parents are very, very upset about the switch to 2 percent milk! We have to do something!"

The person conducting that work, like a school principal, should take the time to investigate the nature and scope of the issue. It could look something like this:

Principal: "Okay, let's talk about this for a minute, I want to understand who is upset and why. How many calls or emails have you received about this?"

Board Member: "I got two calls over the weekend and they said everyone is complaining about the change."

Principal: "Okay, I'm going to put this on our radar to track, and let's check in again tomorrow [or later in the week depending on the board member's patience level] to discuss our options for addressing the issue. In the meantime, please provide me with contact information and I will reach out and talk with them about the issue."

The board member leaves the office knowing that you take the issue seriously and that you are putting in additional effort to discover the scope of the problem. If you discover it really is causing widespread alarm in the community, there will be some options to consider. You can reverse the decision, put together an informational campaign about the change, or something in between. Your data about the communication preferences of your audiences will be one of the first places to turn to let families know where the district is coming from.

If, on the other hand, you discover that the only two calls were coming from parents who were encouraged by a staff person to call because they personally wanted to be able to access the 2 percent milk, you have a completely different communication issue to explore. If you don't take the time to collect the data about an issue, it is impossible to understand what to do next with any confidence.

Once data-driven communication becomes the norm, staff members may even begin to adjust and start to collect information themselves to determine the nature of the issue. This has the potential to cut down on the number of issues that actually make it to the level that requires a school leader's attention.

UNDERSTANDING THE AUDIENCES

Once the nature of the issue is understood, data can also help with identifying the key audiences. Who is most impacted by the issue? Who is influential with those who are impacted? Who has the trust of the most impacted audience? All of these are questions that quantitative and qualitative research can answer.

After identifying the key audiences and influencers, we need to understand the best ways to reach them. While messages are important and identifying audiences are important, determining communication preferences is like building the bridge between the two. A message that is not sent out in the right channel is a lot less likely to reach the target. Paying attention to the analytics on communication systems or asking audiences to self-report their preferences can provide detailed information about how to maximize the effectiveness of the effort.

MEASURING CAMPAIGN EFFORTS

During and after the communication campaign, how do you know if you're successful? Without data, we must rely on anecdotal information from people who are likely already connected to the school and district, reinforcing the things we usually do. Data helps us to get outside of our feedback bubble and hear from people with whom we may not be as connected.

If the Facebook post is lackluster, the data might show us that posts with photos or videos perform much better with our audiences that use social media. If enrollment isn't growing as fast as we expected, the data might show that a significant portion of our potential student population isn't online and needs to be reached in a different way.

Once the campaign is over, data is just as important. If we've set a measurable objective as explained in chapter 6, there is a feedback or behavior target we were striving for in the campaign. For example, the number of new students enrolled in a program, a percent growth in positive perception of the district, or a percent decrease in missed school days. Analyzing our results against the target, the simple answer of meeting or missing the target is easy. What's harder is looking at the reasons why—and that is where the deeper data dive comes in.

Beyond the benefits of communication planning, collecting data allows us to stop guessing and make informed decisions in all areas. Instead of sitting in a leadership meeting and guessing at what might work, or even having heated discussions about the best way to approach a situation based on individual experience that is much more prone to unintentional bias, data shows us the way forward.

It helps us focus our limited time and energy on the things that matter. If one issue is a much bigger issue affecting the community than another that is a pet project, data gives us the argument to focus on the more important issue. If something isn't working or is no longer a helpful communication tool, data gives us the evidence we need to move from one tool to another.

Lastly, collecting data helps us demonstrate the value of school communications and the impact on connectedness and learning. Improving school relationships and engagement is one of the most effective ways of quickly improving academic indicators as well. When families understand a school or teacher's vision and are armed with tools to assist with learning at home, students win. When families' and students' lives are better understood so that schools and districts can provide culturally relevant instruction and communication, we all win.

So while it may appear that adding data collection is adding more work or another step, the reality is that qualifying issues with data collection will ensure that school and district staff are spending limited resources on the most important items and addressing them in the most impactful way.

INTERNAL REFLECTION

To take it a step further, organizational leaders should think about applying data to internal areas as well, for example, an analysis of how money is spent that includes where staff spends their time. It is said that our budget reflects our values, but many times there are issues and areas receiving much more attention and energy than people realize. An audit of how time is utilized in a department can be extremely enlightening.

When the budget is broken up in this way, it can shed a lot of light on the unintended priorities of a school or district. With intentional focus, the attention can shift to other areas or the organization can come to accept the areas that are requiring so much staff time. For example, the department appears to spend the most time and staff resources in the area of school site promotion—something that is very helpful for stakeholders to be aware of, particularly if they are critical of the expenditures in communication. If the promotional efforts result in the recruitment of additional families, the return on investment can be much greater than any financial investment in communication.

DATA SOURCES

When schools and districts begin a conversation about adding research and tracking to their communication and engagement efforts, one of the first barriers is finding the time to add one more thing to an already long to-do list. The good news is that there are a number of ways to conduct research, track your efforts, and evaluate your programs without adding anything new.

Schools are notorious for conducting surveys of families and staff, usually collecting information because a pot of money or program requires data about the impact. Unfortunately, a lot of the time the surveys are being conducted by individuals or groups working in silos, which means the information doesn't get shared across departments, or schools and families get inundated with requests for input and feedback. It's easy to imagine a district where the student services department is collecting school culture information while the curriculum and instruction department is collecting information about the interventions taking place, and the budget department is tracking the specifics of how grant money was spent on afterschool programs and parent training at the same school.

SURVEY LIST

Collecting a list of all the surveys that are taking place in a school is a great way to ensure that data-collection efforts are smarter and stakeholder groups don't get over-surveyed. To start, reach out to staff with a request that they send a list of all survey efforts they lead each year. Ask about the scope of the survey, who is being surveyed, when the survey takes place, the survey format, and the contact information of the person in the school or department who is responsible for the survey or data collection. Add any additional category areas that make sense.

Next, create a centralized spreadsheet list of the district-wide survey and data collection efforts. You may begin to notice some central themes or overlap areas that can be simplified. There may also be a number of people throughout a school or district that are asking for the same information. Perhaps they can share survey tools, methods, and tips.

When all of the efforts are brought together in one place, it is likely easier to see that some populations in the district are given many opportunities to provide feedback and input, while others are not having their voice heard at all. Data gives us the opportunity to dig deeper into our collection efforts. While districts may be doing a wonderful job overall, there may be some stakeholder groups that get left behind, simply as a side effect of the survey tools and methods that are being used. Internet and language accessibility are two of the more challenging barriers to getting full participation and we explore strategies to address them in chapter 4.

When all the data collection efforts are listed together, there will also be a variety of new data sources that can be put to use in communication efforts. Most surveys collect information about how people receive information. Even if that wasn't a question that was asked, many times if a survey was conducted using an online tool, there are analytics that can tell a story about audience preferences. For example, if a district sees a trend of online surveys being answered on smartphones as opposed to desktops or laptops (which is a point of data that some survey tools collect automatically), there are implications for district websites and online publications. When a large majority of stakeholders are accessing material through a mobile device, websites and online collateral should be designed mobile-first: created from a mobile perspective and expanded for other devices instead of the other way around.

That centralized list of surveys is great to have handy when an issue or decision is coming up that needs stakeholder feedback. Instead of creating a completely new survey and going through the effort of marketing that survey, take a look at the list. Perhaps there is a survey that is going out in the immediate future to the same audiences. Simply adding a question or two to an existing survey cuts the workload for everyone involved.

HOW DID YOU HEAR?

Another easy source of data that often gets overlooked is a simple question that can be asked at every event or program registration: How did you hear about this? What's wonderful about this hack is that in addition to being very easy, it also benefits from immediacy and specificity.

Usually, when we are asking people about communication preferences, they are self-reporting, meaning that they are doing their best to remember and guess at the best ways to communicate with them in general. When you ask *as* someone is attending an event or calling to register a student, their recollection of how they heard about the event or program is more likely to be top of mind and accurate.

The results of this kind of effort will point to the communication tools that motivated participants to action, not just those that they are used to seeing on a regular basis. For example, people may be very familiar with the weekly voicemail that their child's principal sends them each week and rate it highly as a method of communication. However, when you compare the summer school registration "How did you hear about this program?" responses, it may be that Facebook was the communication method that actually broke through the noise of all the messages parents receive and motivated them to act and sign their child up for summer school.

RECEPTION LAB

Another simple data collection idea that can help schools clarify issues is to turn the front office into a research lab. Imagine a board member calls with upsetting news. Everyone in town is very upset about the change from whole milk to 2 percent milk and the principal needs to do something about it right away. While it is important to give every concern serious consideration, sometimes a small group of individuals can inflate an issue into something larger simply by calling the right people.

To collect more information about the true impact of an issue, ask front-line staff to keep track of the number of times they are contacted by phone, in person, or by email about the issue. This means keeping a notepad at their desk for a few days to a week and keeping a log of activity. Those numbers can be added to any social media engagement on the topic to come up with a clearer idea of how widespread the "outrage" might be.

BORROW FROM NEIGHBORS

A fourth data source solution that you may not have thought of is borrowing research from other area agencies and businesses. Secondary research, as it is referred to, can contain extremely helpful information that can save schools and districts time and money. A regional government agency is likely attempting to communicate with many of the same stakeholders and if they have already collected information about information preferences and trusted sources, their data can easily be utilized for an outreach plan.

If you are able to develop strong connections with organizations that are reaching out to the same audiences, the same kind of centralized research list could be developed to add even more data sources and opportunities for school efforts. Imagine needing to ask a stakeholder group about internet access or bus ridership and being able to reach out to the local water district and add a question to their survey going out the following week.

In preparation for an effective communications effort, adding a few simple, systemic changes can add a wealth of data for research, tracking, and measuring activities. Easy things like a centralized list of surveys, always asking about how audiences heard about something, and borrowing from other agencies will provide easily accessible information that you can put to use to make your communication efforts smarter and more effective.

ASK & ANSWER

- Do you know the ways your school or district is currently collecting data and how to access it?
- In what areas would better/more data be helpful to you?
- Which of the low-tech data collection methods in this chapter might be useful at your school or district?

SEVENTEEN

Analytics

New principal David Woo understood the value of good school communication. He was always excited to share all the great things happening at Jacksonville Middle School with his parents and community. From the newly renovated gymnasium to the award-winning school band, it was not surprising to see him wandering the halls any day of the week snapping pictures to post to his Twitter account. At the start of the school year he had amassed nearly 350 followers!

However, by the start of spring break Principal Woo noticed that his number of Twitter followers was trending downward with nearly two to three people a day unfollowing him. What was going on? Why were his once enthusiastic followers no longer interested? Seeking answers he enlisted the help of his tech integration teacher Mr. Juarez who suggested they take a look at his Twitter Activity Dashboard for further analysis.

A closer look at Principal Woo's "Top Media" revealed a startling development. On days when he posted six or more times, he lost followers. Mr. Juarez explained that this trend actually made sense because a majority of Principal Woo's followers were students who were interested in hearing about their school but did not want to be inundated with too many posts in a single day. And while there is no specific "rule" for how often to tweet, it appeared that Principal Woo's rapid tweeting was overwhelming his followers resulting in them deciding to unfollow him.

Principal Woo was both disheartened and energized by the news. He was grateful to now have a means of measuring his social media outreach and engagement. Understanding the habits and interests of his stakeholders would help ensure his future success in sharing news about his school.

One of the wonderful things about doing public relations work today is the amount of data easily available through analytics. It may be hard to imagine a world not that long ago in which practitioners had to guess at

145

what the audience was responding to or conduct expensive and time-consuming surveys to get the same information that today is available in a simple click. The challenge is to weed through all of the data now available to get to the numbers that mean the most to your communication efforts.

It can be very tempting to dive down the data hole, get lost in reviewing the statistics, and wonder about the stories they are telling—and that is not a bad thing to do once in a while to ensure you are not missing anything. One helpful approach to analytics is to identify the key metrics that impact public relations efforts and review those key metrics on a regular basis. These metrics will likely point to who is engaging with your school (and who is not), how and when are they engaging, and the type of content they find most engaging. Table 17.1 provides a list of the types of data that can be reviewed for each of these questions.

There are accessible analytics related to websites, social media platforms and tools, e-newsletters, automated call and text systems, online survey tools, and parent portals. While the variety of data available through program analytics is staggering, for the purpose of this book, we'll cover the top three: websites, social media, and e-newsletters.

Table 17.1.

Channel or Tool	Question	Data Examples
Website	Who	Audience, new users, active users
	How	Browser, device, social referral
	Content	Page views, session duration, user flow
Social	Who	Followers, likes, unlikes, reach, fans
	How	Browser, device, top sources
	Content	Reach, clicks, reactions, comments, shares, impressions, visits, mentions, activity
Enewsletter	Who	Deliveries, clicks, open rate, unsubscribed
	How	Browser, device
	Content	Open rate, click rate, distribution, forwards
Survey	Who	Respondents,
	How	Browser, device
	Content	Skipped questions, response rate, completion, visits, time to complete

WEBSITE

If your school or district has contracted with an outside company to provide websites, it is likely that they have their own analytic tools with data that can be shared for the asking. Even if a school or district website is custom or internally developed, it is very easy to add measurement tools. Google Analytics, for example, is free and easy to set up by adding some code to your website. Once installed, Google tracks when your site is visited, the demographics of your visitors, and how they found your page.

Some of the most helpful features or views include User Flow, Site Content, Dashboard, and Mobile Tool. User Flow allows you to see where users started on a site, the pages they visited, and the last page they saw before they left. This data provides rich information about key content areas. For example, if the User Flow shows that many people are coming onto your site from a page other than the homepage, what is the content that is drawing them in—and how can it be featured more prominently?

Site content analytics are a great compliment to the User Flow because this data will help identify the most popular pages and help make that content easily accessible from the main pages of your website and within the navigation. If a significant number of people are moving from the homepage to specific content elsewhere on your site, consider adding that page to a "quick links" section, for example. Your goal, after all, is to make your site as friendly and intuitive as possible so that your visitors find the information they are looking for as quickly as possible.

The Google Analytics Dashboard tool can also be very helpful when set up to reflect your goals and priorities. One of the first items to set is the date range because it is difficult to make assessments about content with short time periods. Unless you are reviewing analytics for a specific event—for example, examining web traffic following a crisis event in your district—set a range of at least a month to have a reasonable portion of data to review. You can provide a unique name for the dashboard, and track new users, number of sessions, and browsers utilized. You can even set up "goals" and measure conversions, or completion rates, for each goal you set up. If Google Analytics has been on the site for a significant period of time, the Dashboard can also help you see and understand trends, comparing previous timeframes to determine improvement.

The Mobile Tool helps you determine what devices your website visitors are using, which has become increasingly important to understand. Whether audiences are experiencing your content on a desktop, on a tablet, or with a smartphone, each device works with websites in distinct ways. For example, if you have a high number of mobile users, you should ensure that your website has a responsive design, or even design for a mobile view first. This data has implications well beyond website design, however, including your approach to creating and organizing content to be easily accessed on the devices your users are most likely using.

While all of these analytics can be helpful and informative, they can no doubt also be a little overwhelming at first. The good news is these tools are useful and accessible for virtually anyone—there is no need for advanced skill sets. Google also offers a free online "Analytics Academy" with a course called "Google Analytics for Beginners." Starting with just a few tools and making time for a little bit of free, online training will ensure you get started in the right direction.

SOCIAL MEDIA

Social media is a powerful tool that is changing the way school communities work, offering a new model to engage with families, staff, students, and the world at large. Pew Research Center studies continue to demonstrate growth each year.

While the national statistics are a gauge of overall use, a school or district's preferences are far more important when it comes to building an effective public relations campaign. When managed strategically, social media conversations help build stronger, more trusting relationships and allow school leaders to have a voice in important discussions related to the work they are doing. If it's not already being measured, it is a good idea to add a question about social media usage to annual school district surveys. This will help school leaders stay current on family preferences—the content your stakeholders want, and where they want to receive it.

Once the school or district identifies the most important social media platforms, setting up the right analytics can assist in ensuring that important audiences are being reached. The key analytics vary by the social media platform. For example, on Facebook, administrators will want to keep an eye on reactions, comments, and shares for each post. Digging deeper, Facebook insights can provide an overview of page activity over a given period of time as well as information on followers, reach, and the demographics of the people who like the school or district Facebook page. One of the most valuable analytics available simply shows what day of the week and/or time of day your followers are most likely to be on Facebook—perhaps the most strategic nugget of data available, when you are trying to decide the timing of your content.

At the post level, the positive reactions, comments, and shares provide good information about the kind of content that page followers want to see. While there may be other types of content that must be shared (operational and safety messages), the positively rated posts can provide examples of the type of content the school or district should post more often to gain additional followers.

On the other side of the coin, posts that draw out negative reactions and comments—or that are shown to prompt followers to hide the post or unfollow your page altogether—can also be very instructive. The comments may tip leaders off to a program, policy, or personnel problem that should be reviewed. It might also provide insight into misperceptions that exist in the community, guiding communication efforts to clear the air and provide accurate information on the topic. While negative reactions and comments should be taken seriously, they should also be understood in the context of the overall percentage of reactions and responses to determine how large and serious an issue it might be. It's natural to focus on negative comments or reactions and fail to see that they are a small minority of the overall engagements. This is no more useful to your strategy and success than focusing only on positive comments and ignoring the negative.

In the page management area of the Facebook, organizations can gain access to invaluable data about their posts and followers, including:

- Published—shows the day and time that a post was published
- Post—small thumbnail and link to the actual post
- Type—indicates what was posted, usually a photo, video, text, or link
- Targeting—who is the post shared with? In most cases, this will be public
- Reach—number of people who saw the post
- Engagement—any action on the post, clicks, reactions, shares, and comments
- Promote—link to pay for promotion of the post

When your posts are listed in the rows to allow for easy comparison in these areas, a number of strategic insights become immediately apparent. As you review, ask yourself these questions:

- What types of posts are receiving the most attention? Check reach and engagement to find them.
- What message or messages are reflected in the top posts? Do they focus on student achievements, staff recognition, or something else?
- What type of content is posted? Are they mostly just text or do they include photos and video? When were they posted?
- Are most of the posts with high reach numbers posted on weekdays, weekends, during the day or evening?

The answers to these questions provide a clear direction for schools and districts to create the most engaging posts and send them out when they are most likely to be seen.

While similar in some ways, Twitter has an additional set of key metrics that can shift your use from tactical to strategic and valuable. There are three main areas to find useful analytical data—the Account Home, Activity Dashboard, and Audience Insights Dashboard. The Account Home provides a great overview of information, including:

- Impressions—measurement of the total number of views of a conversation
- Profile Visits—number of times users visited your profile page
- Mentions—every time username is tagged on Twitter with the @ symbol
- Followers—number of users who are following the account

It also has a "Tweet Highlights" section that lists the Top Tweet (with the most engagement), Top Mention (someone else's tweet that mentions your account), and Top Media Tweet (tweet that includes a photo or video). While the highlights section reflects just the last twenty-eight days, it is a good idea to take note of any themes in the content types that receive the most engagement because this can guide your content decisions moving forward.

The Tweet Activity Dashboard contains a section that is very similar to Facebook's Overview Page, listing all the tweets in the past twenty-eight days in a table format that makes it easy to compare different tweets for impressions, engagements, and engagement rates (number of engagements divided by impressions). These numbers are important because they tell a story about the intensity of interest in the content. A tweet might be seen by a lot of different people, but if they don't feel compelled to interact with it, the tweet will have a low engagement rate. A large reach with low engagement isn't necessarily a bad thing, but remember that your top social media goal should always be engagement.

Instagram and LinkedIn also contain analytical dashboards that can be scanned for insights. There are also a number of scheduling tools, such as HootSuite, Buffer, and Sprout Social, that allow administrators to manage multiple social media accounts and pre-schedule posts, while also providing a wide variety of meaningful analytics.

While all of this data is very helpful to understand your audiences' engagement behaviors, it can be overwhelming to get started. The important first step is to understand what social media platform your audience is already using—and to share there. Not only will those posts and tweets help you gain followers and build a social media community, but the data they generate will give you a baseline to review. Once the data begins to roll in, the social media analytics will start to provide actionable information. There is no shortage of support for those hoping to collect and understand social media analytics. Whether free tutorial videos and articles, or paid services, it is worth your time to learn about the social media work you are doing—what's working, and what can be improved to maximize your investment of time and effort.

E-NEWSLETTERS

There are a number of e-newsletter programs available for schools and districts, and they generally offer similar analytic information. The most important data questions you should ask with an e-newsletter begin with how many of your families and stakeholders have an email address to receive your e-newsletter, and the internet or smartphone access to read it. If these are barriers for even a small percentage of the population, it is important to choose an e-newsletter tool that also allows you to print out copies to provide to those audiences.

Once the e-newsletter is sent out, there is a wealth of data that will start to collect:

- How many people the e-newsletter was sent to
- How many people it didn't reach (bounce-backs due to blocked programs or incorrect e-mail addresses)
- How many people opened the e-newsletter (open rate)
- How many people clicked on links provided in the e-newsletter (click rate).

In addition, many e-newsletter programs also feature more sophisticated information, including the browsers and devices readers are using, when and who they forward the e-newsletter to, if they open it more than once, and when they open it.

Most commonly, open rates reflect the success of the subject line you use for your e-newsletter. Focus on words that will engage a busy parent, spark curiosity among your audience, and entice them to open that email. Schools and districts may want to try a number of different approaches to increase the interest in opening the e-newsletter, from the basic "ABC Unified E-newsletter September 2018" to highlighting different items in the newsletter, like "Catch Up on Girls Soccer Highlights in This Month's E-newsletter" or "Jefferson Elementary Captured a Top STEM Award, Find Out How!"

Understanding click rates tells you a lot about what your readers are most interested in learning more about. Consider including the first one or two paragraphs of a story in the newsletter, and link to the rest of it on the website or social media page. When someone is interested enough to find out more, that clicked link becomes part of your data set and can be compared against the click rates of other items in the e-newsletter that month or any month.

In summary, because so many of our communication systems have moved to digital formats, data collection has become easier and cheaper. When leaders are looking at the right data, they can make the best decisions possible about where to spend their limited time and budget in connecting with stakeholders. It is worth a little time now to analyze information that can save schools much more in the long run.

ASK & ANSWER

- What systems are you already using that have analytical data that can be accessed?
- What additional tools or systems might you start using so that you can better track your communication efforts?
- If you are already collecting analytical data, can you identify any themes or trends related to topics, tools, or audiences?

Part V

In Closing

EIGHTEEN

Leading

Schools are a reflection of the community around them. A campus deals with the same challenges, biases, and conflicts that occur in the region and country. As the leader of the school, society's issues are your issues. You may not be able to solve everything, but awareness and attention to these topics may minimize the impact they have on your students and staff.

As discussed in the introduction of this book, the current educational environment is fraught with inequity, polarization, and mental health challenges. Ignoring these issues doesn't make them go away and can in fact make them worse. When a leader doesn't directly address something, it can send the message to the team that the behavior is acceptable and lead to more of that behavior.

Collecting data is one way to ensure that all members of the school community are being held to high standards. While not perfect, data is less likely to be impacted by personal relationships and implicit bias. For example, a teacher may be so charming and friendly with the principal and staff that it is hard to imagine that he could be failing to connect with students. However, a school climate survey would make it clear that his students are far less likely to report feeling connected to their teacher and the school.

Data can also point to the inequities on a campus. Looking at outcomes for students and comparing those outcomes with other factors affecting their experience can help to identify the barriers that cause achievement gaps. Once the challenges are clear, they can be addressed. For example, schools can work on providing training around bias, exploring wraparound social services and school based health centers, expanding mental health access, and working to become more culturally responsive at all levels.

CHALLENGING CONVERSATIONS

Some of these issues will start with difficult conversations. Today's leaders must be ready to lead those conversations and not let fear of controversy lead to avoidance. As with produce, crucial conversations are better earlier.

Crucial Conversations: Tools for Talking When Stakes Are High by Patterson, Grenny, McMillan, and Switzler demonstrates that these kinds of conversations can be anxiety provoking but necessary. Issues like race, inequity, and mental health can cause people to be defensive, angry, or even shut down. The book's authors argue that there are four key questions to ask when embarking on a crucial conversation to ensure it is more effective:

- What do I really want for myself?
- What do I really want for others?
- What do I really want for the relationship?
- How would I behave if I really wanted these results?

Asking these questions allows a leader to mitigate the anxiety they might be feeling and steel themselves for potentially challenging interactions. For example, when leading a discussion about adding more culturally responsive enrichment materials to the school's English curriculum, a principal might find herself facing a room of upset teachers.

They may feel the idea is an attack on their professionalism or an accusation of racism or bias and raise pointed concerns and questions. The four questions above help leaders pay attention to the feelings beneath the words, moving past attacks to work towards the desired results.

It is also important to model the behavior you want. People will listen to what you say, but only when it matches what you do. In fact, what you do as a leader is far more powerful than what you say. Your decisions, your budget, your hires, and your vulnerability tell the true story of your campus values and vision.

LEADING ON RACE AND EQUITY

While equity should be part of every aspect of leading schools and is included in many of the chapter discussions, it is a fact that some school leaders try to avoid the potential for controversy when talking about race.

Let's be honest, it is difficult for most people to acknowledge and address issues related to racism and equity. It can be challenging, intimidating, and fraught with tension. However, as a powerful influence in your community, it is critical for school leaders to be aware of how race impacts schools on a variety of levels. Finding the courage to address it takes planning, practice, and persistence.

For example, are you and your staff aware of any implicit bias you may have about people of different races? That may be a tough question to answer because much of our conditioning around race is to make it wrong to pay attention to it. A healthier approach is to be curious about bias, and want to know in order to recognize and neutralize it as much as possible. School leaders must shift their paradigm from "Am I a racist?" to "How can I grow and actively cultivate a school environment that reflects diversity and values equity?" and "How can I help my community advocate for and implement anti-racist policies?"

A good place to begin is by asking yourself tough questions. What don't you know? Are you tuned in to the subtleties of systemic racism and bias that don't allow you to see past your belief systems? How aware is your staff about what is happening in the neighborhood, community, and even across the nation, that may be impacting students and staff of color?

For example, the Black Lives Matter movement was founded in 2013 in response to the killing of black teenager Trayvon Martin. Since that time, BLM has grown worldwide resulting in unprecedented youth activism in response to social justice issues. However, in some districts and schools, teachers and administrators who struggle with how to engage the topic have decided to simply ignore it.

Unfortunately, when refusing to acknowledge this seminal moment in American history, schools lose the opportunity to educate and inspire students and staff of all races to understand the importance of social justice, activism, and advocacy. Children watching recent protests and clashes with police on television need schools to help them understand and process what is happening. Education provides the dual benefit of not only providing context to help them make connections but also teaches students the importance of social responsibility. Experts agree that talking about racism and race with young children is the best way to encourage inclusion and equity.

In the book *Cultivating Genius*, Dr. Gholdie Muhammed argues that too often in our classrooms, the challenges of people of color are studied, but rarely do we study their joy. Beyond activities associated with cultural celebration months, school leaders should consider whether or not their school's curriculum highlights the positive achievements of people of color. This audit should extend to the selection of texts and multimedia pieces from diverse authors, musicians, scientists, historians, and so on. *Cultivating Genius* is a great resource for educators looking to expand their teaching practice to be more culturally responsive.

Ultimately, school leaders have to assess if their students and families feel that their needs are being met in a way that acknowledges and honors their home life and culture. Bringing a diverse team together to talk about these issues can help bring unknown challenges and opportunities to light. It is not an easy conversation, but it is a necessary one.

BARRIERS

There are a number of reasons talking about race and equity can be tough. For one, groups of people may start with a different set of facts. The US is increasingly polarized, as are our information sources. Depending on where someone is getting their news, people who share similar values may enter a conversation with a completely different perspective on a given issue.

In addition, most people lack the knowledge or training to assess and address issues of race and equity. For many of the reasons discussed in this book, educators and organizations are reluctant to dive into these issues. Unfortunately, this becomes a vicious circle because the less that people learn about these areas, the less able we are to discuss and address them.

For some, there is resistance to bringing up the topic because of the fear of backlash. How will they be perceived if they are the "trouble-maker" asking questions about such a sensitive topic? In a defensively minded system, it can be a risk to professional relationships, upward mobility, or even someone's current position to question the status quo.

On the other side of the coin, people may also be fearful about offending the groups that have systematically been oppressed. What if a leader brings up the issue and somehow does it in the wrong way? What if they say the wrong thing or act in the wrong way? What if instead of bringing people together, it rips the community apart? Most of these concerns have to do with the unwillingness to risk discomfort. Race is such an incendiary topic that people feel that discussing it will risk their personal or professional status and relationships.

In addition to the fear associated with race and equity, there are significant differences in people's perceptions about the topic. Each person has a kind of virtual backpack they carry around with them that has formed the person that they are. This backpack includes a person's demographics, including where they were born and raised, their socioeconomic status, and ethnicity. It also includes their lived experiences and the media that they consume. Lastly, it includes the influences of their family of origin and educational experiences.

All of these things come together to inform a person's perspective on the world, including race. With so many diverse backpacks in the world, it should come as no surprise that people look at issues so differently. Understanding that diversity of perspective can help guide productive discussions.

TALKING ABOUT RACE

If your school or district has a strategic plan or statement on equity, that can also be a great starting point. What does the statement say and what does it mean to the people in the room? Do you have the right people in the room to represent the wide variety of perspectives on race and equity issues? Digging deep to understand these plans and statements and the promise they are making to students, families, and the community can help bring everyone together with a common goal.

The other important element to review is the school, district, and community data related to race and equity. Look at a variety of quality of life factors, because all of these areas impact students. How are people of color in your community faring in the areas of housing, healthcare, mental health, internet connectivity, employment, and childcare?

Take a look at community assets like schools, parks, libraries, grocery stores, banks, and transportation. Do communities of color have the same practical access to these necessities? How do these areas impact families and students' ability to show up ready to learn?

It can be tempting to look at race and equity in schools with a narrow lens of test scores, attendance, and punishment. In many states, that is all that is required to be responsive to equity concerns. But looking at those items is like a doctor documenting the systems of a disease and prescribing aspirin to decrease discomfort, but not addressing the foundational issue.

The foundational equity issue in schools is that achievement gaps are caused by many factors happening outside of schools. That does not mean it is out of the school's ability to address those issues. It means that a school leader must think more broadly and systematically about how to address them to truly bring equity to their school. That means bringing in the data and bringing in the partners in the community that can help.

As disagreements arise, and they will, continue to bring the conversation back to students and how to ensure that they are receiving the equity promised in the school, district, and community language.

STARTING A HEALTHY DISCUSSION

A framework for healthy planned and informal discussions is the CARE Model:

- Consider the Context
- Act with Courage
- Reflect Without Judgment
- Expect Discomfort

First, consider the broader context in race and equity discussions. In planning conversations surrounding these topics, it is necessary to view racism as trauma. Medically, trauma is defined as what happens after you experience an event or events that hurt you physically or emotionally. However, in a very real sense for people of color, the persistent micro and macro-aggressions faced over time as a result of racism can be seen as traumatic. This can bring on symptoms such as fear, anger, anxiety, hopelessness, hypervigilance, and mistrust.

As you begin planning your discussion, remember it's important to educate yourself and your staff to help them understand the current climate and nuances at play when discussing race. If a person of color was recently killed by police in a neighboring city, students, staff, and families of color may be justifiably on edge. Consider your relationship with the person you are talking with as part of the context. Have you built up enough trust to ask for their vulnerability?

The second element, acting with courage, is about taking proactive steps to interrupt racist talk and actions. If someone is making a racist joke or comparison, it can be awkward to call it out, but that is exactly what is needed. Pointing out a racist statement or action is not about calling the person a racist or making them wrong—it is about everyone growing in their knowledge about racism, which is all around us.

Acting with courage is about challenging racial assumptions whether they are happening at a dinner party or the decision-making table. How did someone reach that conclusion? What set of facts are they working with to make that statement? Acting with courage is also about questioning racist outcomes. Gaps in achievement, health care access, and quality childcare point to inequitable systems.

Ultimately, acting with courage is about making yourself vulnerable and being willing to risk your personal and professional comfort. People of color do not have a choice to opt out of racist systems or about being the target of racist language and actions. Courageous leaders join communities of color in that struggle because they are committed to equity for students and families.

The third element is reflecting without judgment. There may be times that you or someone else in your organization will intend to communicate one thing and it will mean something else to different groups. It's natural to feel defensive and cling to the explanation that it is what was intended that matters and that the other group is too sensitive or wrong in some way. However, this third element is about reflecting without judging and that means owning the *impact* of what is said or done rather than arguing about whether or not someone else's experience is valid.

Some tips that help in this endeavor include *blameless autopsies*, assuming good intentions of others, and identifying the emotion behind words or behavior. A blameless autopsy is about reflecting on an interaction or even a crisis situation to objectively identify what happened and how it impacted a variety of groups.

Bringing representative advisors together to talk about the incident can be particularly insightful. Ask, "I know we meant ____, but what some people heard was _____. How do we do better?" Listen to their perspectives about the larger context that could have made the difference between what you meant and what was understood. It is also important to forgive yourself for honest mistakes that are made along the way and do better the next time.

Expecting discomfort is the fourth element of the model. Authentically talking about race and ethnicity is hard and uncomfortable. It is natural to not know exactly what to say or to feel shame for saying the wrong thing.

It is also part of the process to feel attacked and expecting to feel that way can help avoid defensive responses and instead dig deeper into that feeling and where it originates. Going through these kinds of discussions will cause discomfort as we question existing beliefs and when we feel that we are risking some relationships. All of these feelings are normal.

It can be helpful to step away from a discussion when you are feeling that you might react defensively and instead acknowledge the vulnerability it took for the other party to share their discomfort. For example, saying, "I appreciate you sharing that, and I/we want to do better."

If you are actively engaged in anti-racist and equity work in education, you will not be perfect. You will not encounter people at their best. These issues are intense and threatening. The important thing is to always remember who you are there to serve. If your thoughts, words, and actions are in service to students, you may stumble but centering students will always help you move forward on the right path.

TAKING CARE OF YOURSELF

Leading a school community is a huge responsibility and requires a great deal of time and energy. Given the number of challenges that campuses are facing, an effective leader must meet them with resilience and a positive attitude. That mindset can be maintained with a few healthy habits.

While the job often requires an intense focus, it is helpful to also know when to let it go. Stepping away from the mental burden of leading a school community, whether it be for a walk, a weekend, or a vacation is imperative and can lead to breakthroughs on tough issues. There will always be more to do in a school community, always another email to read or to send, another meeting to schedule or attend, another phone call to answer or make. There is only one of you though, and the more balance in your life, the stronger your resilience.

Connecting with peers can be another form of briefly stepping away with the benefit of strengthening the team. Education is not for the weak of heart and getting together to commiserate over challenges and celebrate small wins can do wonders for morale, even if it is over a small break at a coffee cart.

Connecting with students is a surefire way to feel reinvigorated. Feel frustrated, exhausted, or stuck? Step into a classroom and interact with a student. Read a book or observe an art lesson or math discussion. Immersing yourself in the learning your hard work supports for even just fifteen minutes can refresh your attitude dramatically.

Developing and maintaining health habits is also critical to a positive mindset. Making time for enough exercise and sleep can be tough, but not getting enough of either of those will eventually affect your performance as a leader. Drinking plenty of water throughout the day and ensuring that you are fueling yourself with food that provides plenty of nutrients is also part of the effectiveness equation. It is hard to be present and truly listen to students, staff, or community members when you are exhausted.

Keep work away from your personal life as much as possible. Your smartphone already provides emergency email, phone, and text access just about everywhere you go. Be protective of the time you have with family and friends; it is another way to feed your spirit and ensure that you have something to give to the job when you return.

Lastly, keep in mind that good people make mistakes. Part of staying resilient enough to continue to serve your school community is forgiving others when they fall short of your expectations. Don't take it personally and leave room for grace and moving forward. More importantly, forgive yourself when things go wrong. Figure out how it happened and resolve to do better next time.

As President Theodore Roosevelt remarked famously, "The credit belongs to the man who is actually in the arena, whose face is marred by dust and sweat and blood; who strives valiantly; who errs, who comes short again and again, because there is no effort without error and shortcoming; but who does actually strive to do the deeds; who knows great enthusiasms, the great devotions; who spends himself in a worthy cause; who at the best knows in the end the triumph of high achievement, and who at the worst, if he fails, at least fails while daring greatly."

ASK & ANSWER

- What data is available to me to understand more about equity in my school community?
- Who can I invite to a discussion on race and equity to bring a unique perspective to the table?

- What community issues are creating barriers to learning at my school?
- What community assets are available to help?
- How am I modeling what I want for my students?

Appendix A

Online Supplemental Materials

There are a variety of *The Communicating Principal* supplemental resources available, including training materials for those who want to train their teams and templates that leaders can put to work on their communication campaigns.

Materials are located at: www.schoolprpro.com/the-communicating-principal.

Training Materials

- Research (Chapters 2 & 3)
- Planning (Chapters 4, 5, 6)
- Social Media (Chapter 8)
- Crisis Communication (Chapter 10)
- Customer Service (Chapter 14)

Templates and Examples

- Survey Outreach Plan Template (Chapter 2)
- Survey Questions (Chapter 2)
- Simple Communication Plan Template (Chapter 5)
- Communication Plan STEM example (Chapter 5)
- Campaign Plan Case Study (Chapter 5)
- Communication Options Example (Chapter 9)
- Communication Worksheet Template (Chapter 9)
- Example Key Messages and Speaking Points (Chapter 10)

Appendix B

Employee, Community, Family, and
Student Engagement Ideas

Superintendent's Advisory Council: Leaders representing a variety of neighborhood, ethnic, and community groups that advise on issues and concerns.

Superintendent's Representative Council: Invite a representative from each school site and district department to participate in regular meetings for classified and certificated staff to share concerns and assist in problem-solving.

Superintendent's Student Cabinet: Student leaders from each school meet quarterly with the superintendent to discuss campus-level concerns and provide feedback and ideas on new district initiatives.

Facility Advisory Groups: Collaborative meetings of employee, administration, and community members who meet to analyze budgets, space at area schools, and make recommendations on actions that improve cost savings and/or learning environments.

School Site Council: Each school incorporates a site council made up of families and staff to assist the principal with important campus decision-making.

District Advisory Council: Invites a parent representative from each school site to meet with district leadership, provide feedback on district initiatives, and make suggestions for improvement.

District English Learners Advisory Council: Advisory body for English learner families serving a role similar to a District Advisory Council.

Budget Advisory Committee: Community members and employee representatives review the district budget to ensure responsible spending.

Parenting Classes: Certified staff provide trainings that offer family members positive approaches to parenting, for example Parent University.

Family Involvement Retreats: Invite school staff representatives and parent leaders to participate in semi-annual planning sessions to review academic data, intervention funding plans, and parent engagement opportunities.

Neighborhood Celebrations: Every spring, invite everyone in the community to the local high school campus to celebrate outstanding employees, students, retirees, and volunteers.

Welcome and Wellness Fair: Employees are welcomed back to the school year with an event that introduces central office departments to employees through interactive booths, and showcases local organizations and businesses that promote a healthy lifestyle.

Administrator Hiring Input Sessions: As new administrators are hired at the district and school level, stakeholder groups involving a variety of teachers, students, families, classified staff, and other administrators have provide guidelines and feedback on candidates.

Teacher and Classified Employee of the Year Interview Panels: Invite members of the community and staff representatives to sit on the panel used to select district employees of the year.

Task force groups: Invite community members to participate on groups related to budget cuts, school consolidations, curriculum review, parent engagement, facility improvements, the achievement gap and teacher and principal effectiveness.

Glossary

While readers may be aware of these words and phrases in other contexts, this glossary provides guidance on how they are used within the school communications field.

Anecdotal a specific incidence that may or may not be representative of a larger group.

Ambassadors people who are connected to the school system and are willing to help communicate about issues and promote school programs within their personal and professional networks.

Analytics the demographic, reach, and engagement numbers that are associated with various digital communication platforms like social media, websites, and email.

Audience the key people who need to receive the message to make the campaign successful.

Brand the whole of the experience that stakeholders have with a campus or leader, including service, cleanliness, communication effectiveness, and more.

Campaign collection of activities based on research and planning that are designed to create change, also referred to as a communication effort.

Channel the method of communication that allows a school leader to get a message to stakeholders/audiences.

Collateral materials that are created to support a campaign.

Content the messages that are created to communicate about school information and events.

Crisis an interruption to the campus environment that requires a leader's immediate attention and response.

Effort	the whole of a series of actions that assist in getting a message to stakeholders in a variety of ways, also referred to as a campaign.
Engagement	capturing the attention of campus stakeholders to the point that they react with the messages, for example, commenting on a social media post.
Evaluative Research	collecting information after a campaign to help determine its success as well as provide guidance for future campaigns.
Formal Research	research that is structured in an objective way that gets the same result when replicated.
Formative Research	research that helps determine the direction, audience, messaging, and tactics of a campaign before it starts.
Four-Step Public Relations Process	a framework that provides the optimal process for public relations/communication campaigns. Under the RPIE model, the steps are research, planning, implementation, and evaluation. Under the RACE model, the steps are research, analysis, communication, and evaluation.
Hashtag	preceded with a "#" in social media, it is a phrase that helps organizations track all the conversations using the same phrase or caption.
Impressions	number of times that a message is viewed.
Informal Research	anything that someone does to learn more about the audiences, issues, strategies, and tactics that could be used in a campaign.
Measurable Objective	specific goal set for the change you want to see in a campaign.
Message	the key words or phrases that persuade the audience to do or think about something.
Platform	usually referring to something that is digital, it is the channel that someone might use to send out messages. For example, Facebook is a social media platform.
Practical Access	beyond technical or theoretical access to a message or a tool, practical access considers the practical barriers that impact the ability of some groups to access some messages.
Primary Research	research that the organization does itself.

Protocol	list of agreed-upon guidelines for a process.
Qualitative Research	research about issues that are difficult to quantify. It may include observation of behaviors, interviews, focus groups, and more.
Quantitative Research	research about things that can be quantified, for example surveys with demographic and multiple choice options.
Reach	how many people have been exposed to the message.
Representative	when something applies to the experience or perception of a larger group.
Respondent	someone who replies to a survey.
RPIE	one model of the four-step PR process: includes research, planning, implementation, and evaluation.
Secondary Research	research that another organization has conducted but that is useful for a campaign, for example census information.
Stakeholder	anyone that is connected and/or dependent on an organization. For example, students, family members, teachers, support staff, board members, and community leaders are examples of a school's stakeholders.

Additional Resources

- Free templates and training materials related to this book (https://www.schoolprpro.com/the-communicating-principal)
- Racial Equality Resource Guide: www.racialequityresourceguide.org
- Dual Capacity: https://www.dualcapacity.org/
- Violence Prevention: www.cdc.gov/violenceprevention/aces

ORGANIZATIONS

- SchoolPRPro (schoolprpro.com)
- National School Public Relations Association, NSPRA (nspra.org)
- West Ed (wested.org)
- Teaching Tolerance/Learning for Justice (learningforjustice.org)
- Harvard Implicit Association Test (https://implicit.harvard.edu/implicit/takeatest.html)
- Racial Equality Tools (racialequitytools.org)

TEXTS

- *How to be an Antiracist*, by Ibram X. Kendi
- *White Fragility*, by Robin DiAngelo
- *Cultivating Genius: An Equity Framework for Culturally and Historically Responsive Literacy*, by Gholdy Muhammad
- *The Power of Moments*, by Chip and Dan Heath
- *Teach Like a Champion 2.0*, by Doug Lemov
- *Five Dysfunctions of a Team*, by Patrick Lencioni
- *My Grandmother's Hands: Racialized Trauma and the Pathway to Mending Our Hearts and Bodies*, by Resmaa Menakem
- *Visible Learning for Teachers: Maximizing Impact on Learning*, by John Hattie
- *Engaging Data: Smart Strategies for School Communication*, by Trinette Marquis
- *Crucial Conversations Tools for Talking When Stakes Are High* by Patterson, Grenny, McMillan, and Switzler

SOCIAL MEDIA

- *Social Media Imperative: School Leaders and Strategies for Success*, by Kristin Magette
- https://www.begindot.com/ways-to-increase-facebook-reach/
- https://later.com/blog/ultimate-guide-to-using-instagram-hashtags/
- https://help.twitter.com/en/using-twitter/how-to-use-hashtags#

About the Authors

With more than twenty years experience in communications, marketing, and public relations, **Trinette Marquis** is passionate about working with public schools and improving school community relationships.

Early in her career, she worked with Fortune 500 companies, statewide nonprofits, and internet start-ups but realized something was missing. Inspired by her father's positive experience as a custodian, Trinette brought her business talents to the schools where she grew up and eventually started her own communications consulting business in 2012 to help districts throughout the country.

Her work has been recognized by the National School Public Relations Association, the American Association of School Administrators, the Medical Marketing Association, and the International Association of Business Communicators. She is past president of the California School Public Relations Association and regularly presents to national audiences on public relations. Trinette is also a part-time professor of communications at California State University, Sacramento and American River College. She is the author of the book *Engaging Data: Smart Strategies for School Communication*.

When she's not talking about school communication, you'll find her working out with her Kaia tribe, hiking in Northern California with friends and family, or enjoying the garden with Bill and their dog Bernie.

Natalie A. Nash, MSC, began her career in news reporting as news assistant at the *New York Times*/Chicago Bureau working alongside Pulitzer Prize–winning journalist Isabel Wilkerson. Later, as communications manager for Deborah's Place, Chicago's largest provider of supportive housing for women, she served as liaison to the Mayor's Office of Special Events where she coordinated media relations for the Illinois Coalition to End Homelessness. In 2005, she became the Director of Communications at Crete-Monee School District 201-U, a suburban unit district thirty-five miles south of Chicago.

She believes that the new imperative for today's communications professional is to help create school environments that provide a positive framework for critical conversations, particularly around race, culture, and equity. In 2014, she was invited by the Illinois Association of School Administrators (IASA) to write about her work with crisis communication following the protests in Ferguson for their *Leadership Matters* publication. Her work has been honored with multiple awards from the National School Public Relations Association.

Natalie is a national presenter and currently serves as co-chair of the INSPRA Equity Task Force where she works with school PR professionals from across the state of Illinois to promote, empower, and create equitable practices relevant to the role of the school communications professional.

She is happily married to Steven and they reside in Chicago with their daughter, Vivian.